AF323392

How to Draw Exotic Flowers Volume 2 (This Book on How to Draw Flowers Includes Easy to Draw Flowers Through to Hard to Draw Flowers)

This how to draw flowers book contains advice on how to draw 20 flowers quickly step by step

---

James Manning

How to Draw Exotic Flowers - Volume 2

Introduction

Drawing stimulates parts of the brain that are responsible for creative thinking and imagination. From a young age, we are all creatively encouraged to draw, often to improve our fine motor skills and co-ordination.

From toddler 'scribbles' to 'matchstick men' you may find that as you get older you will want to tackle more complex drawings (perhaps it's an image you have seen in a book) but as you begin to put pencil to paper you may have no idea where to start, causing you frustration and annoyance.
With the help of our 'How to Draw' book series, this frustration will disappear as we guide you step by step, line by line, to create your very own masterpieces!

Each illustration in this book is deconstructed and simplified into lines and shapes that will not overwhelm you. As we guide you to form each simple line and shape together on the paper, the image gradually becomes more detailed and textured.

There will be such a sense of accomplishment and achievement once your drawing is complete, which in turn will boost your self-esteem and confidence.

Drawing Characters Step-by-Step

For the rest of the book I will show you how to draw 20 different drawings step by step. Each step will build on the previous step until eventually you have 20 complete drawings. The illustrations that I detailed on the previous pages will be included within these characters so please look out for them.

If you would like to download the outline sketches for any of the characters I have made an additional book with all of them inside. You can download this for free by visiting the web address below:

https://www.lipdf.com/product/flowers2/

If at first, you find my step-by-step approach too complicated or difficult please leave it to one side and come back to it later. Instead, use the grids with numbers and letters on it first. By following the coordinates and matching them up with the coordinates on a blank grid you can redraw the characters that way instead.

What to do if you get frustrated whilst drawing

You may find that whilst working through my 'How to Draw' series, you may become frustrated as you find learning the new skill harder than you may have first anticipated. What you have drawn on the paper may be different to how you envisioned it to look, or you may be constantly comparing your skill to friends and siblings efforts. Learning a brand new skill can be difficult and time consuming, and you will need to remind yourself that everyone learns and works at different paces and that it is perfectly fine for you to take your time in refining your new skill.

If you find that your concentration is lost and you become agitated and frustrated with your work, it is very important to try and keep the activity fun and engaging, so encouraging regular breaks is imperative. It may even be better to encourage yourself to do a completely different activity for a while and come back to drawing tomorrow.

Validating your feelings is also crucial. It is okay for you to feel annoyed and frustrated, but always encourage yourself to keep trying.

Perhaps tell yourself to take a step back in the book and repeat a part that they you have already mastered, then gradually move onto the step that you are finding trickier.

Everyone, including adults and the most successful artists can make mistakes, and sometimes these mistakes could even be successes! The extra line or shape you may have drawn accidently, could become part of the drawing as a whole and copying the lines exactly as they are in the book isn't a necessity.

However, drawing in pencil, rather than permanent ink, allows any 'mistakes' to be erased and learnt from. Being able to remove what you feel is a mistake will stop you from feeling overwhelmed and that you must start over from the beginning; instead you can carry on from the point you were able to erase out.

Try to always reinforce to yourself that the best way to learn when drawing is to learn from mistakes and continue on.

James Manning, ClinPsyD

HOW TO DRAW FLOWERS - VOL 2

Here are all of the drawings in this book. I guess it must seem like there is a lot of them when they are looked at all at once!

Luckily, I am not going to ask you to draw them all straight away. The best way to learn to draw is one step at a time. Each drawing in this book may require between 50 and 200 strokes of your pencil, but all you will need to think about is drawing one stroke at a time.

As you use your pencil, stroke by stroke, working your way through this book, you will eventually be able to create all of the drawings!

Drawing Step-by-Step

In this book I will show you how to create 20 different drawings step by step. Each step will build on the previous one until eventually you have 20 complete drawings.

To make things easier for you, please download the outline grids for the drawings. You can download this additional book with all of them inside for free by visiting the web address below:

https://www.lipdf.com/product/flowers2/

At first, you find my step-by-step approach too complicated or difficult please leave it to one side and come back to it later. Instead, you may want to use an alternative grid with numbers and letters on it first. By following the coordinates and matching them up with the coordinates on a blank grid you can redraw the pictures this way instead.

I have put details below about where you can download these basic grids for free on the internet.

https://www.lipdf.com/product/grids/

You can of course ask an adult to help you draw the grids instead, or you may even feel able to draw them yourself.

Please see page 40 for the webpage address for your bonus books and the password.

1. Although this is the first drawing in the book, you don't have to start drawing here! Flick through the book and find your favourite drawing to start with.

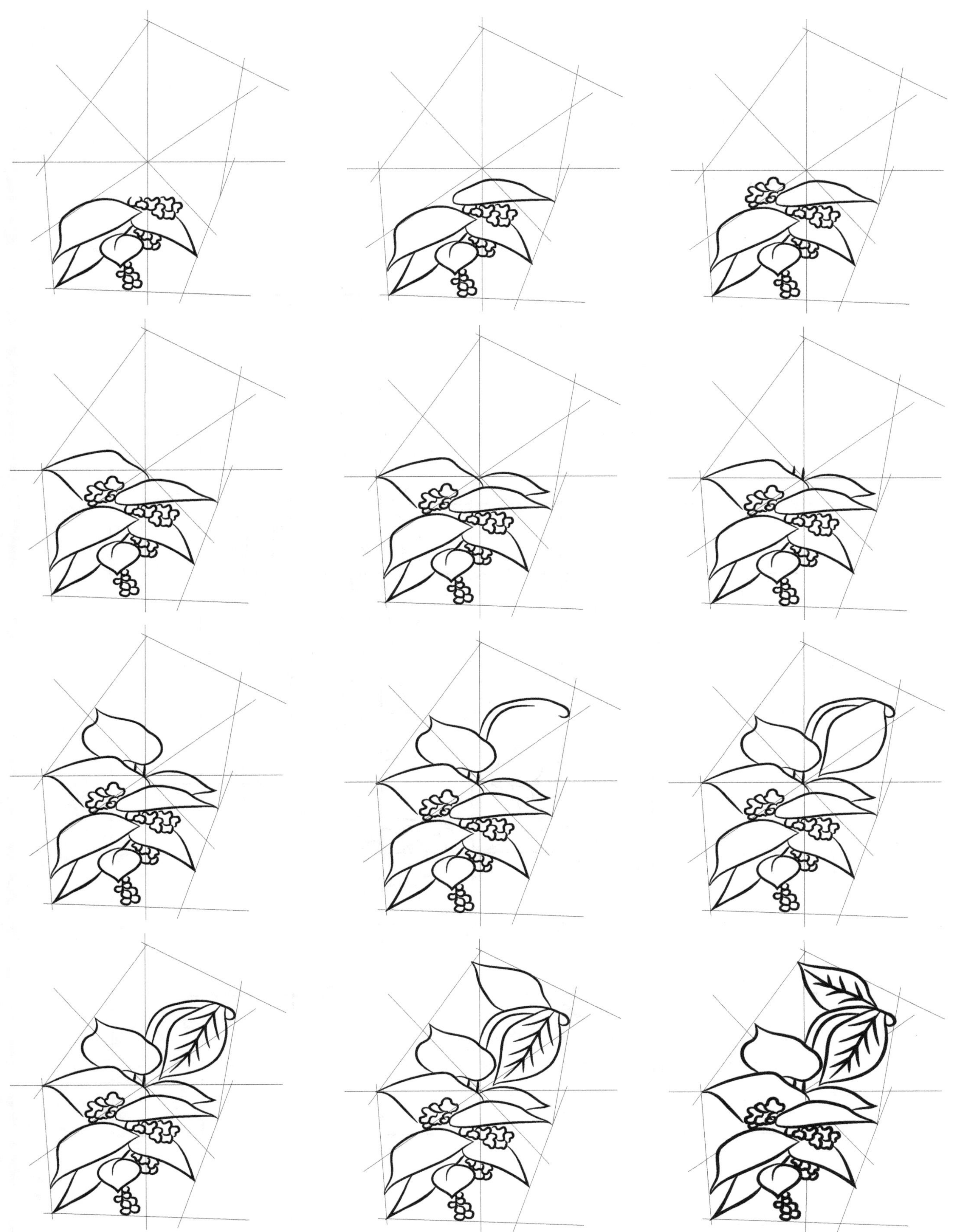

You can download blank grids to practice with in dark and light PDF formats by following the link below.

https://www.lipdf.com/product/grids/

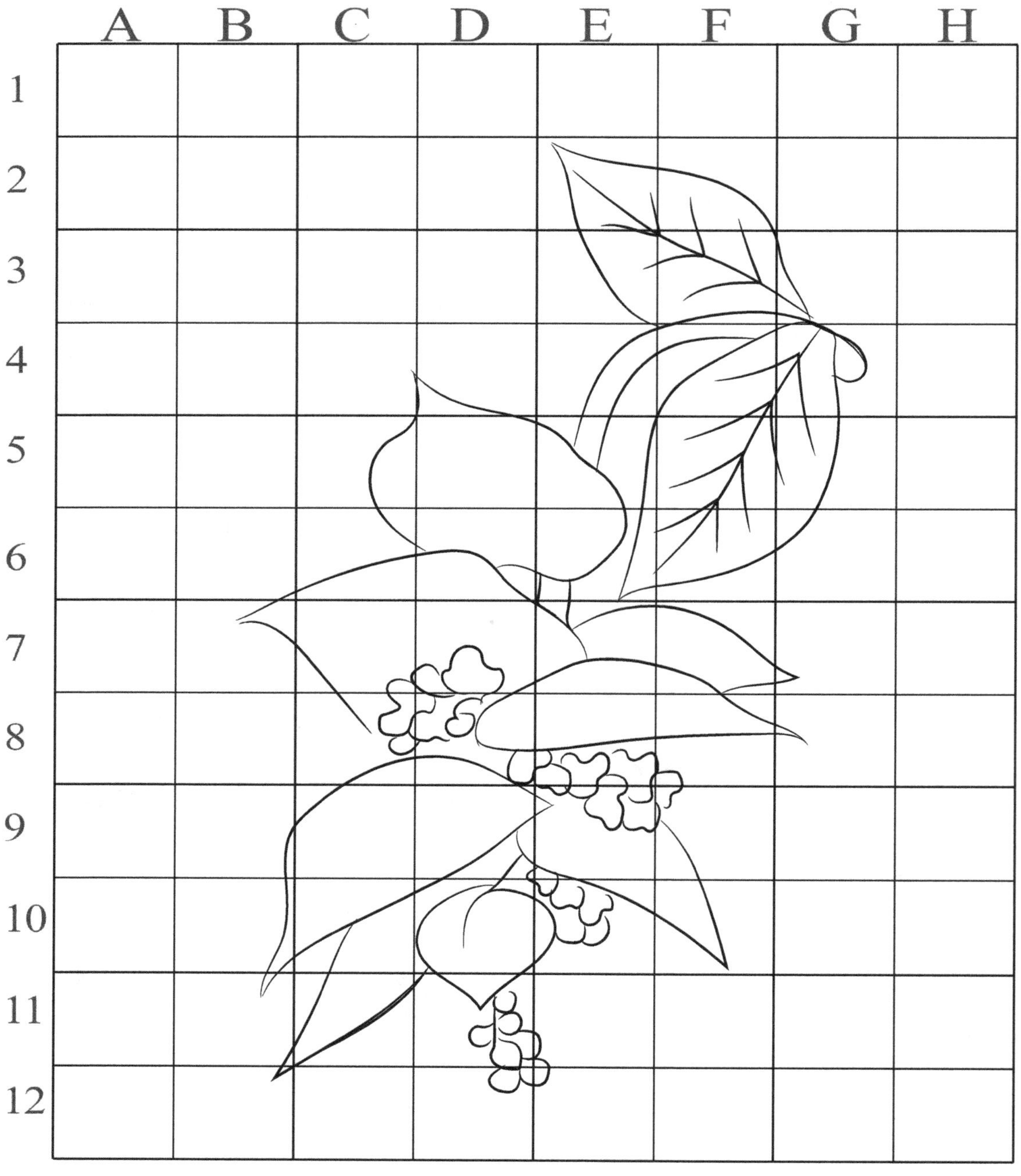

2. Try not to sketch using a pen as you will be unable to erase any mistakes. It's often helpful if you use a pencil so you can erase anything you think is a mistake.

Suggested outline sketch

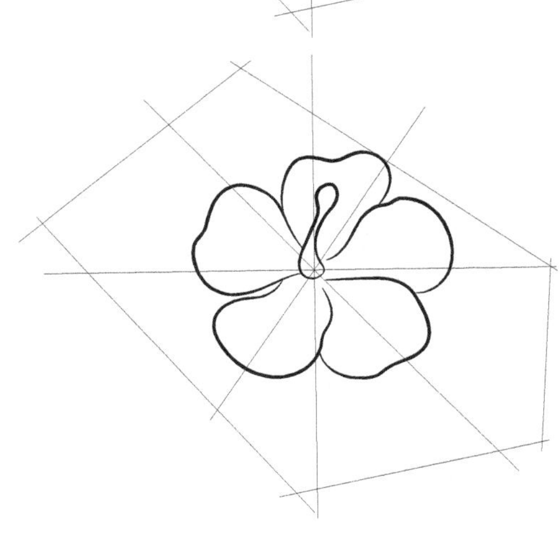

You can download blank grids to practice with in dark and light PDF formats by following the link below.

https://www.lipdf.com/product/grids/

3. The first stroke of your pencil can often be the most daunting but give it a go and see where the drawing takes you!

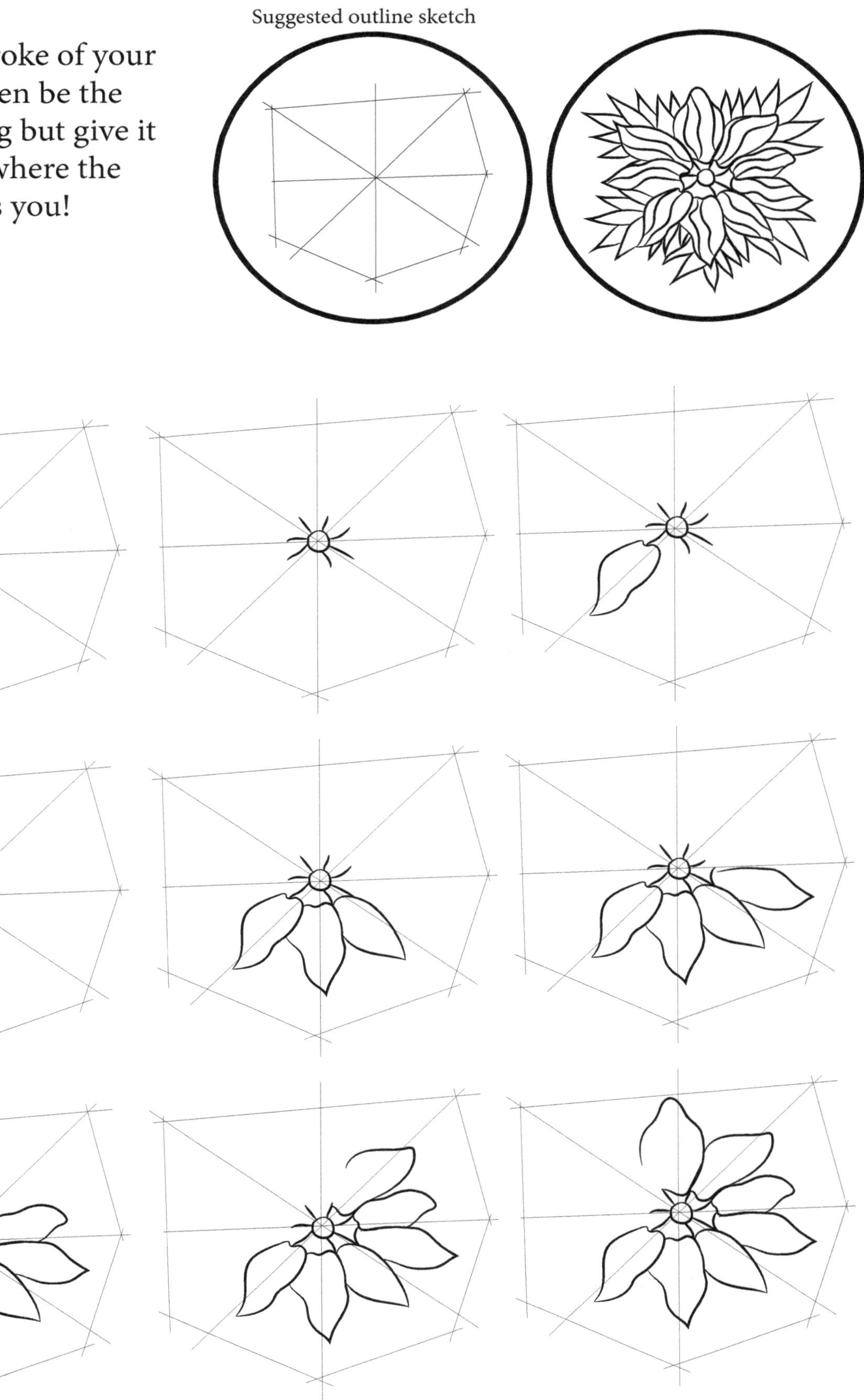

You can download blank grids to practice with in dark and light PDF formats by following the link below.

https://www.lipdf.com/product/grids/

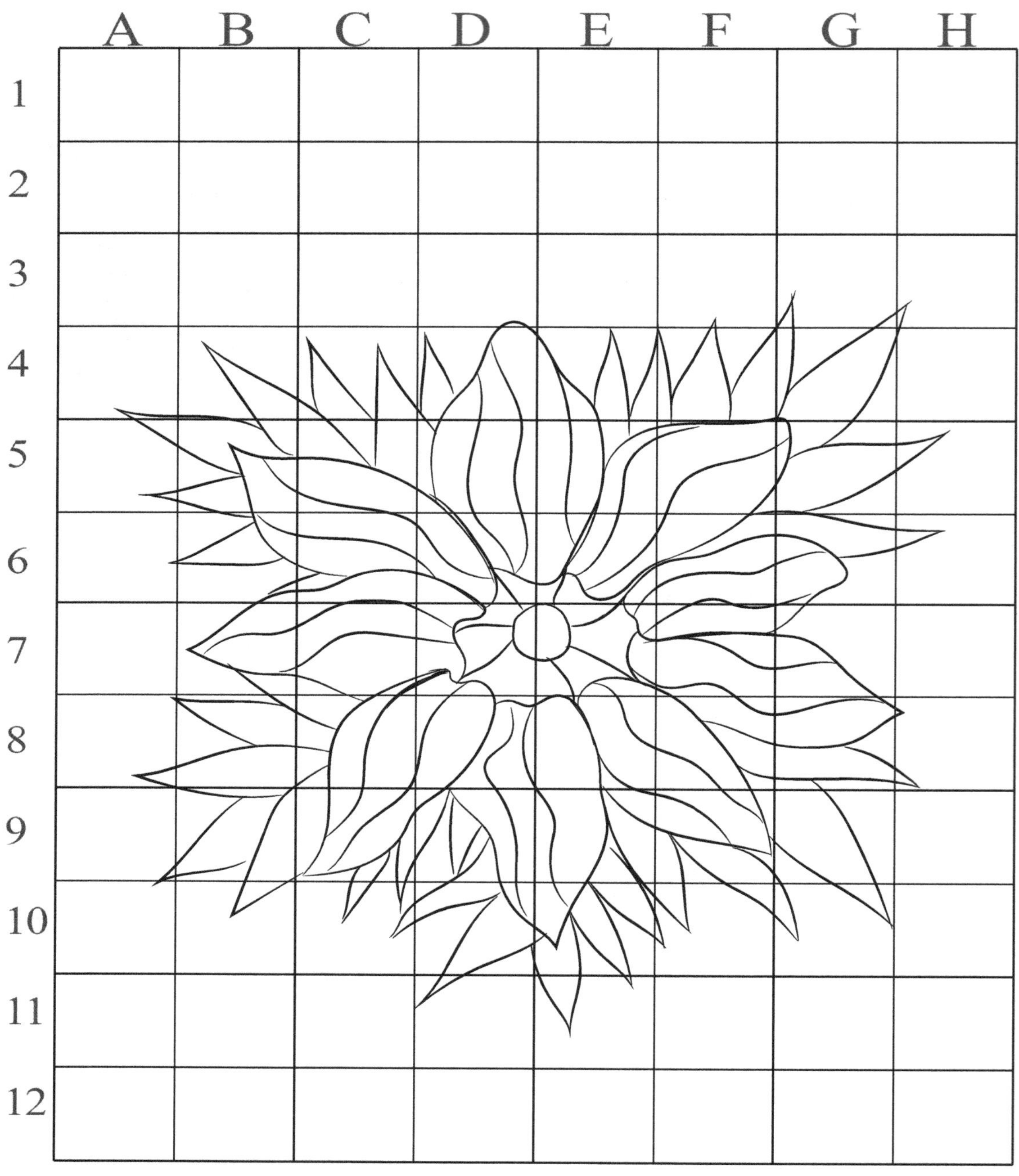

4. Copying the lines exactly as they are shown in the book isn't a necessity, use the grids as a guide and source of inspiration for your own drawing.

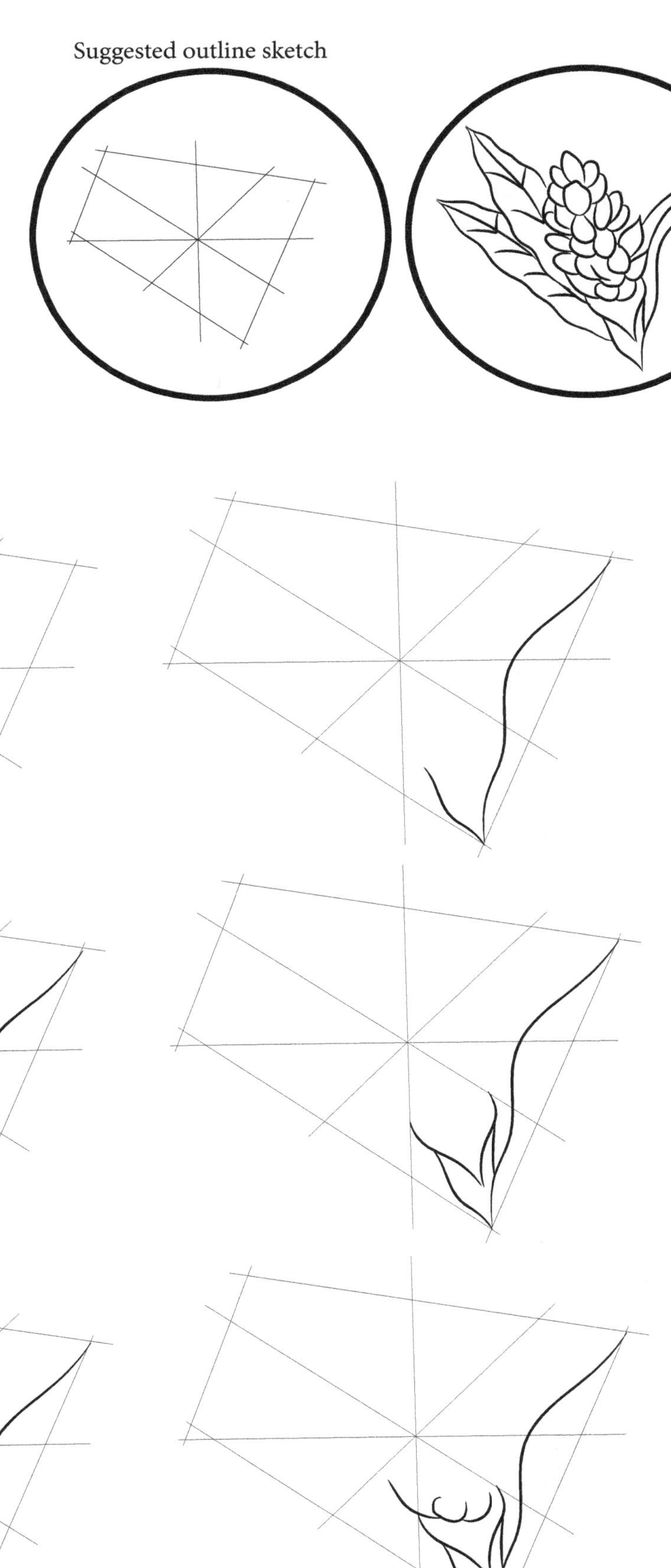

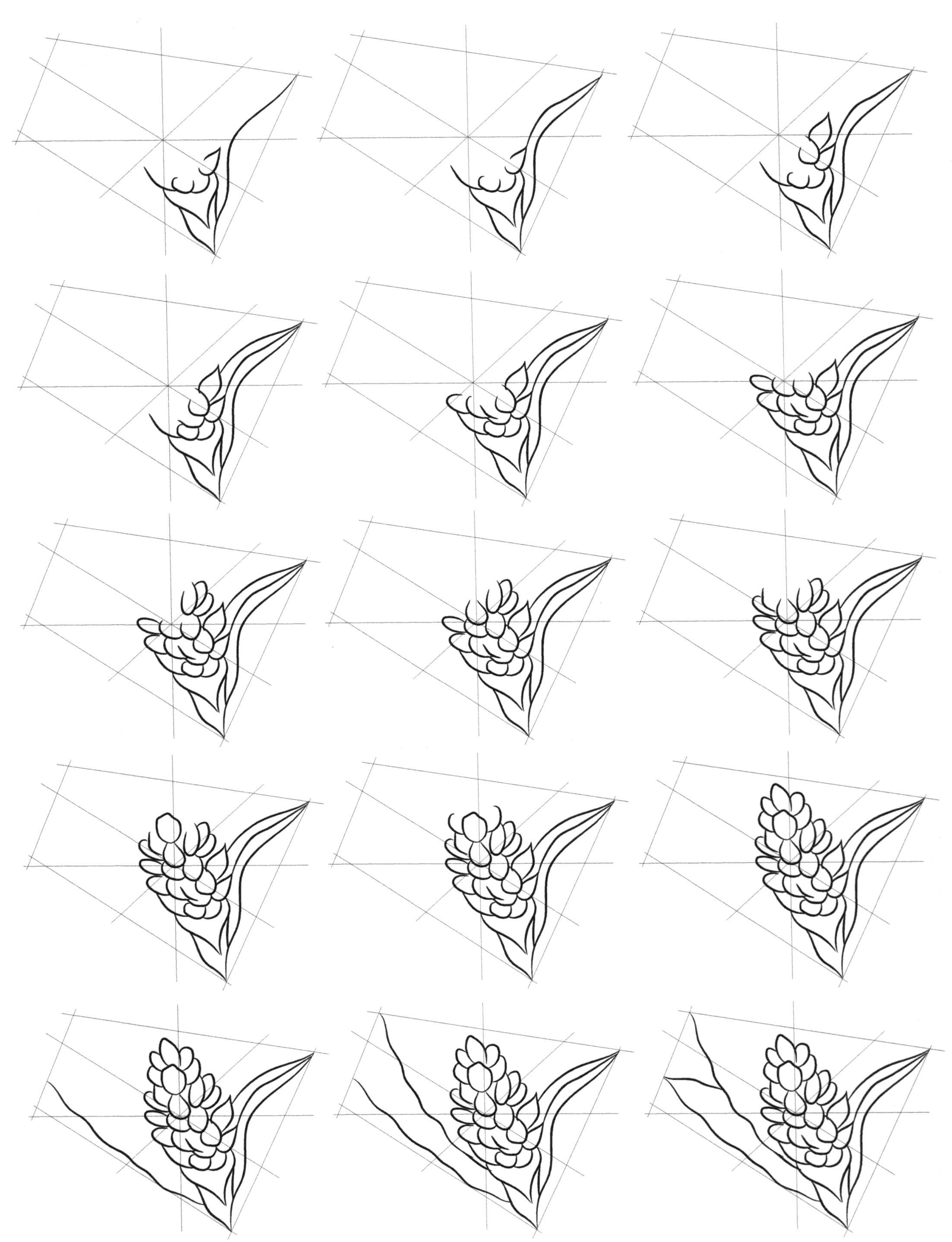

<table>
<tr><td></td><td>A</td><td>B</td><td>C</td><td>D</td><td>E</td><td>F</td><td>G</td><td>H</td></tr>
<tr><td>1</td><td></td><td></td><td></td><td></td><td></td><td></td><td></td><td></td></tr>
<tr><td>2</td><td></td><td></td><td></td><td></td><td></td><td></td><td></td><td></td></tr>
<tr><td>3</td><td></td><td></td><td></td><td></td><td></td><td></td><td></td><td></td></tr>
<tr><td>4</td><td></td><td></td><td></td><td></td><td></td><td></td><td></td><td></td></tr>
<tr><td>5</td><td></td><td></td><td></td><td></td><td></td><td></td><td></td><td></td></tr>
<tr><td>6</td><td></td><td></td><td></td><td></td><td></td><td></td><td></td><td></td></tr>
<tr><td>7</td><td></td><td></td><td></td><td></td><td></td><td></td><td></td><td></td></tr>
<tr><td>8</td><td></td><td></td><td></td><td></td><td></td><td></td><td></td><td></td></tr>
<tr><td>9</td><td></td><td></td><td></td><td></td><td></td><td></td><td></td><td></td></tr>
<tr><td>10</td><td></td><td></td><td></td><td></td><td></td><td></td><td></td><td></td></tr>
<tr><td>11</td><td></td><td></td><td></td><td></td><td></td><td></td><td></td><td></td></tr>
<tr><td>12</td><td></td><td></td><td></td><td></td><td></td><td></td><td></td><td></td></tr>
</table>

5. If you find you are
getting frustrated with
your drawing, take a
break and come back to
it later.

22

You can download blank grids to practice with in dark and light PDF formats by following the link below.

https://www.lipdf.com/product/grids/

6. Don't worry if you are spending more time drawing a picture, it's more important to take your time when producing high quality work.

Suggested outline sketch

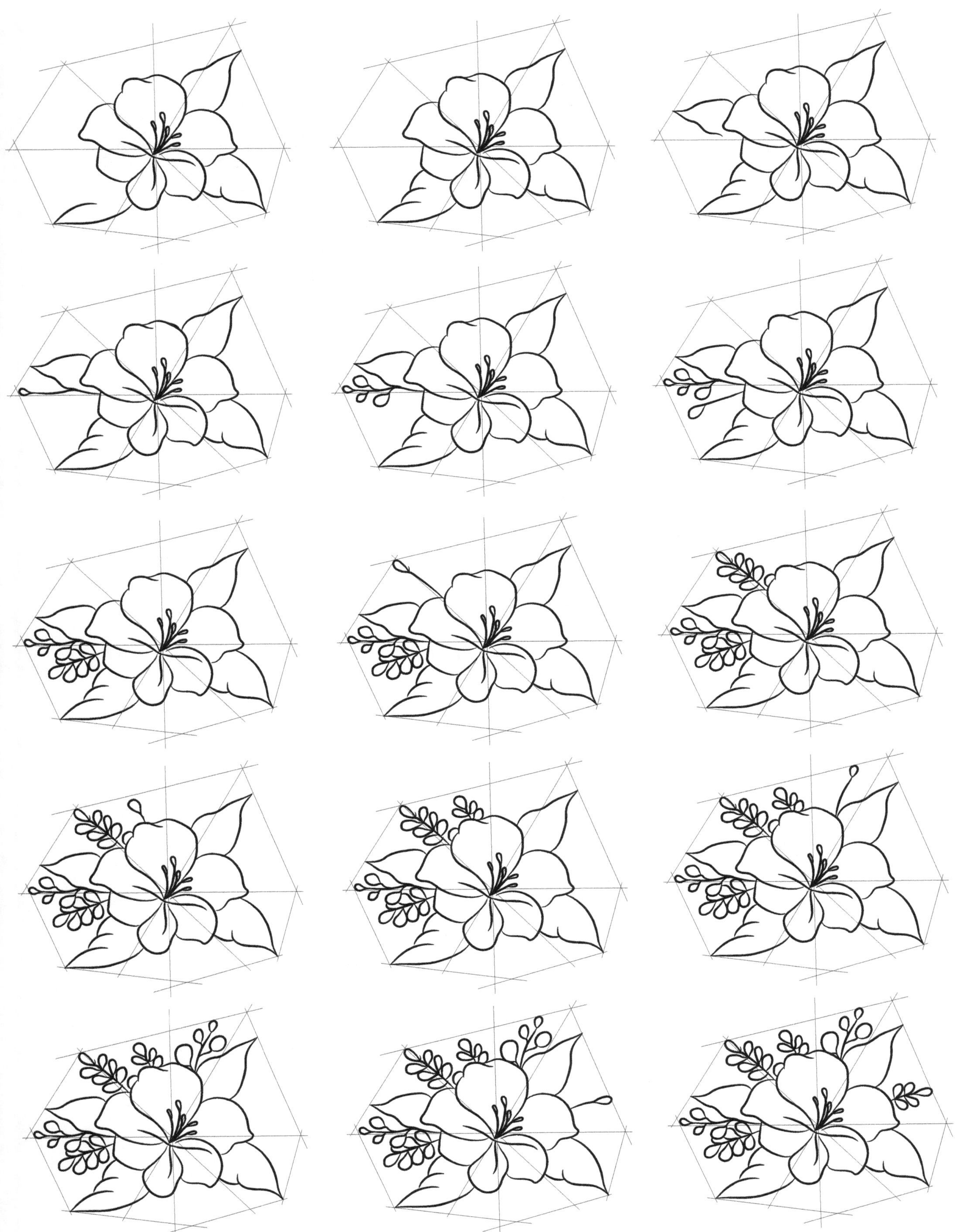

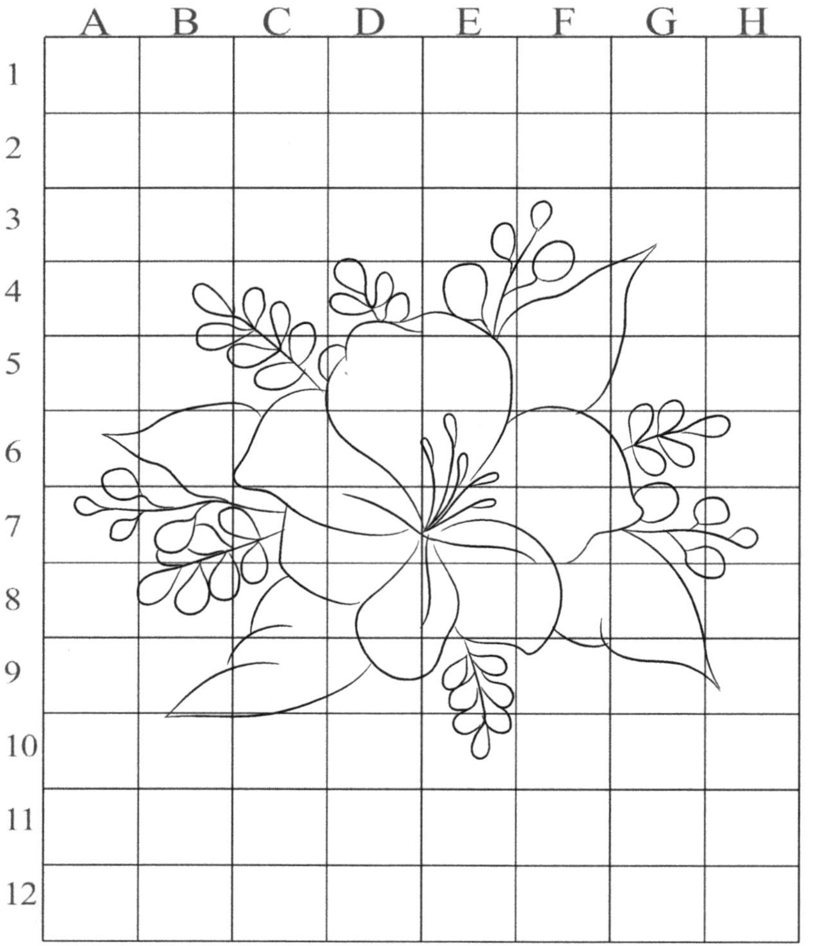

A B C D E F G H
1
2
3
4
5
6
7
8
9
10
11
12

7. Don't forget the outline sketch is there to help you. Use it to help keep your drawing in proportion.

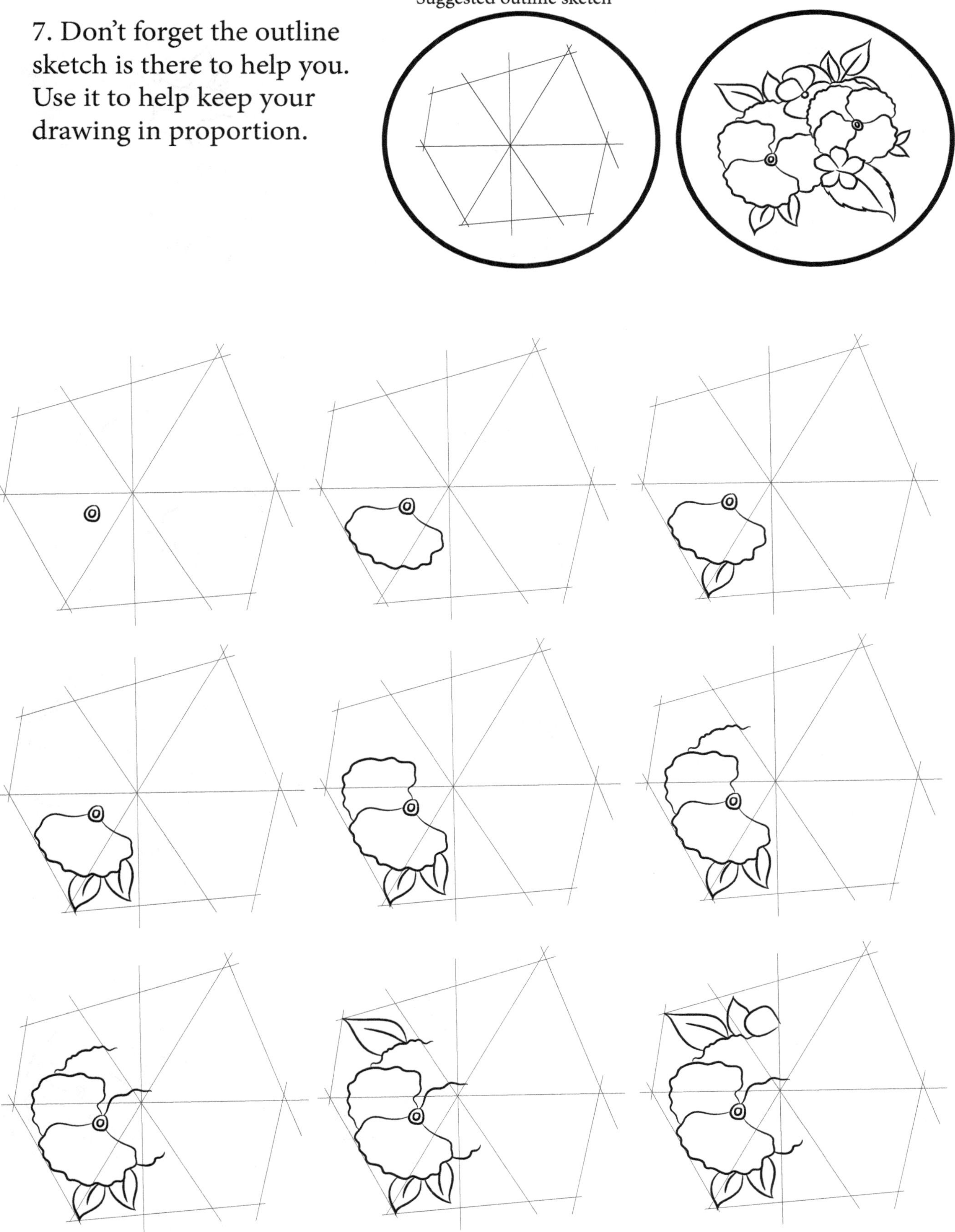

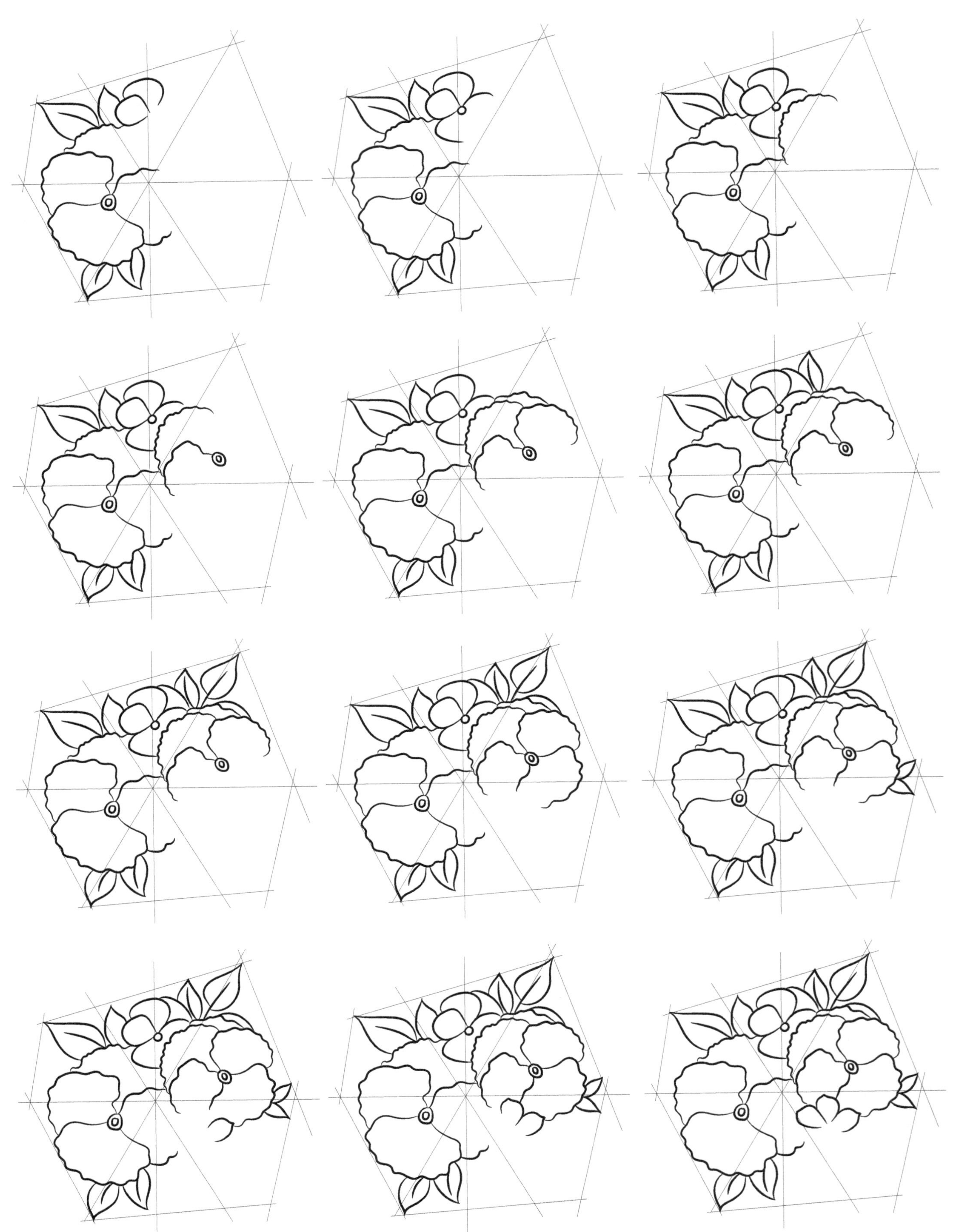

You can download blank grids to practice with in dark and light PDF formats by following the link below.

https://www.lipdf.com/product/grids/

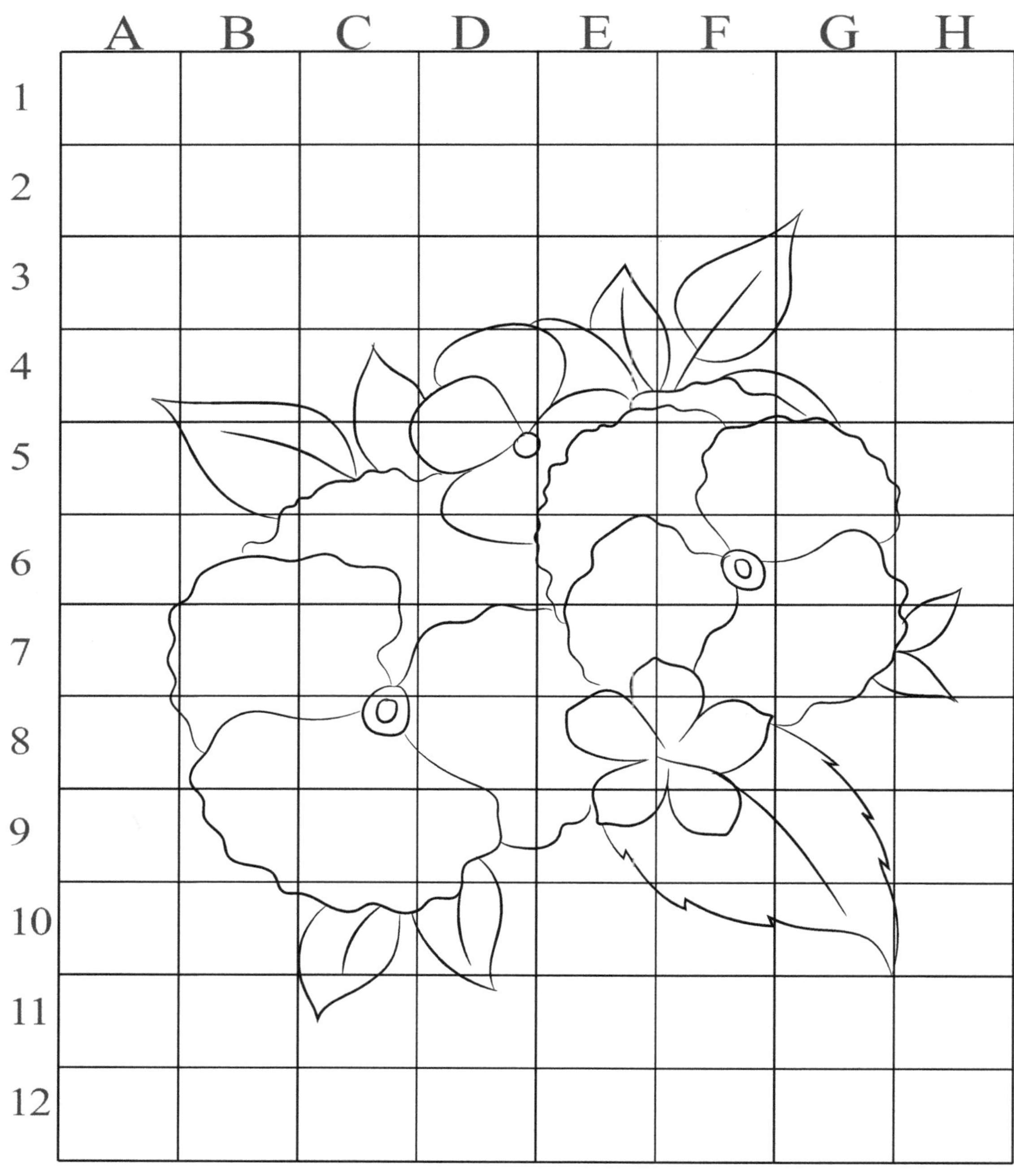

8. Add some colour to the finished drawing to really give it some personality.

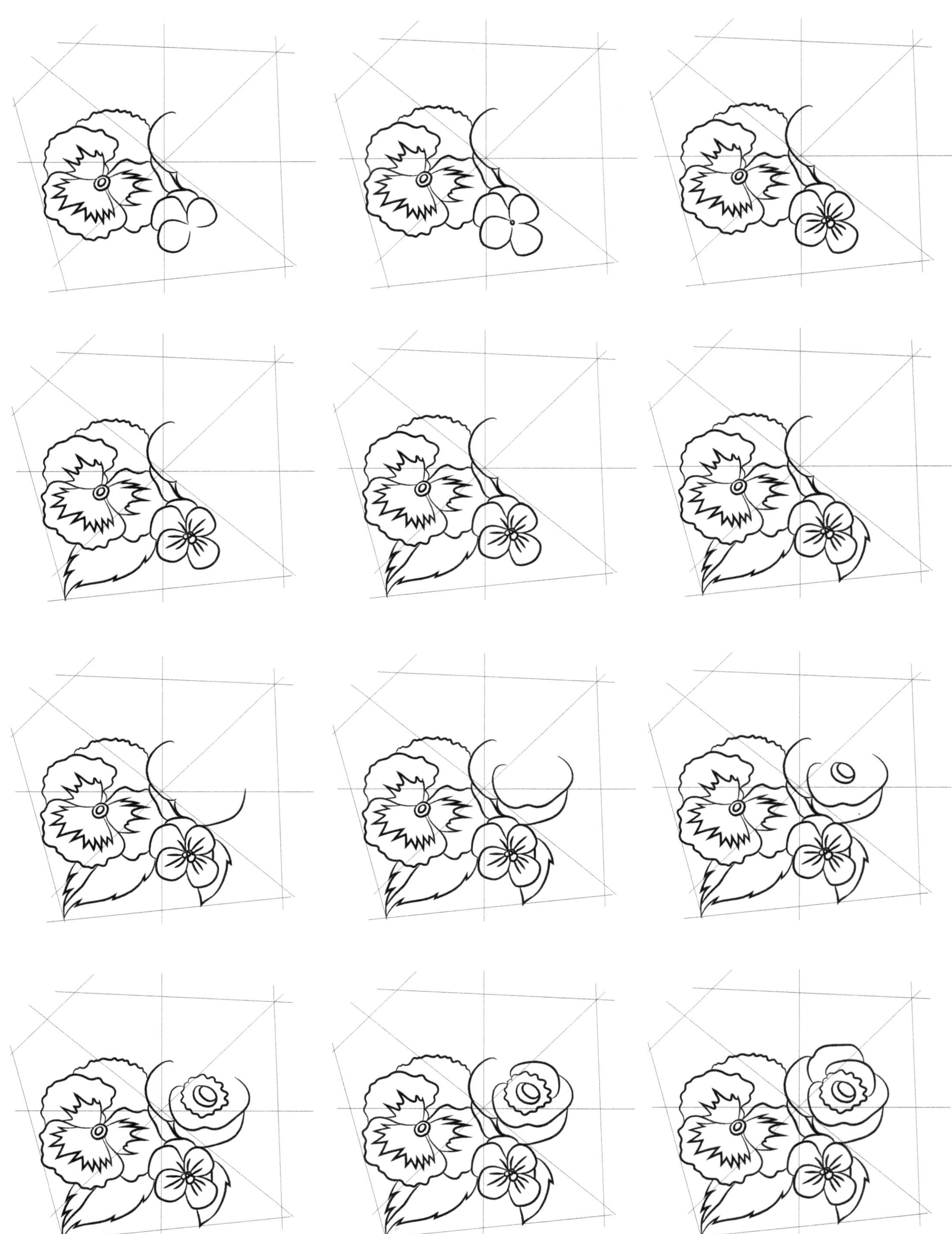

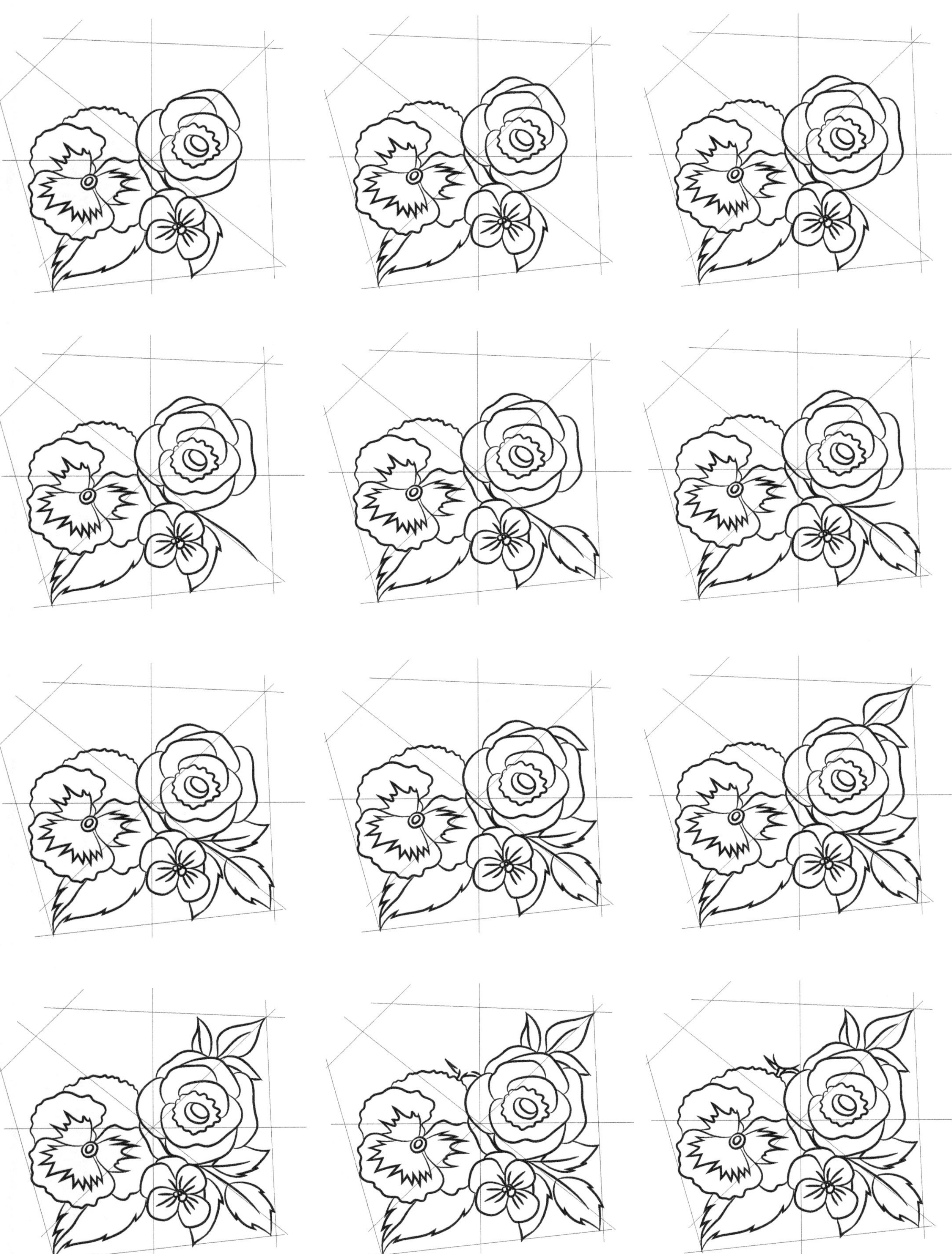

You can download blank grids to practice with in dark and light PDF formats by following the link below.

https://www.lipdf.com/product/grids/

9. Why not experiment with how you hold your pencil? How you hold a pen for handwriting may not be comfortable for drawing.

Suggested outline sketch

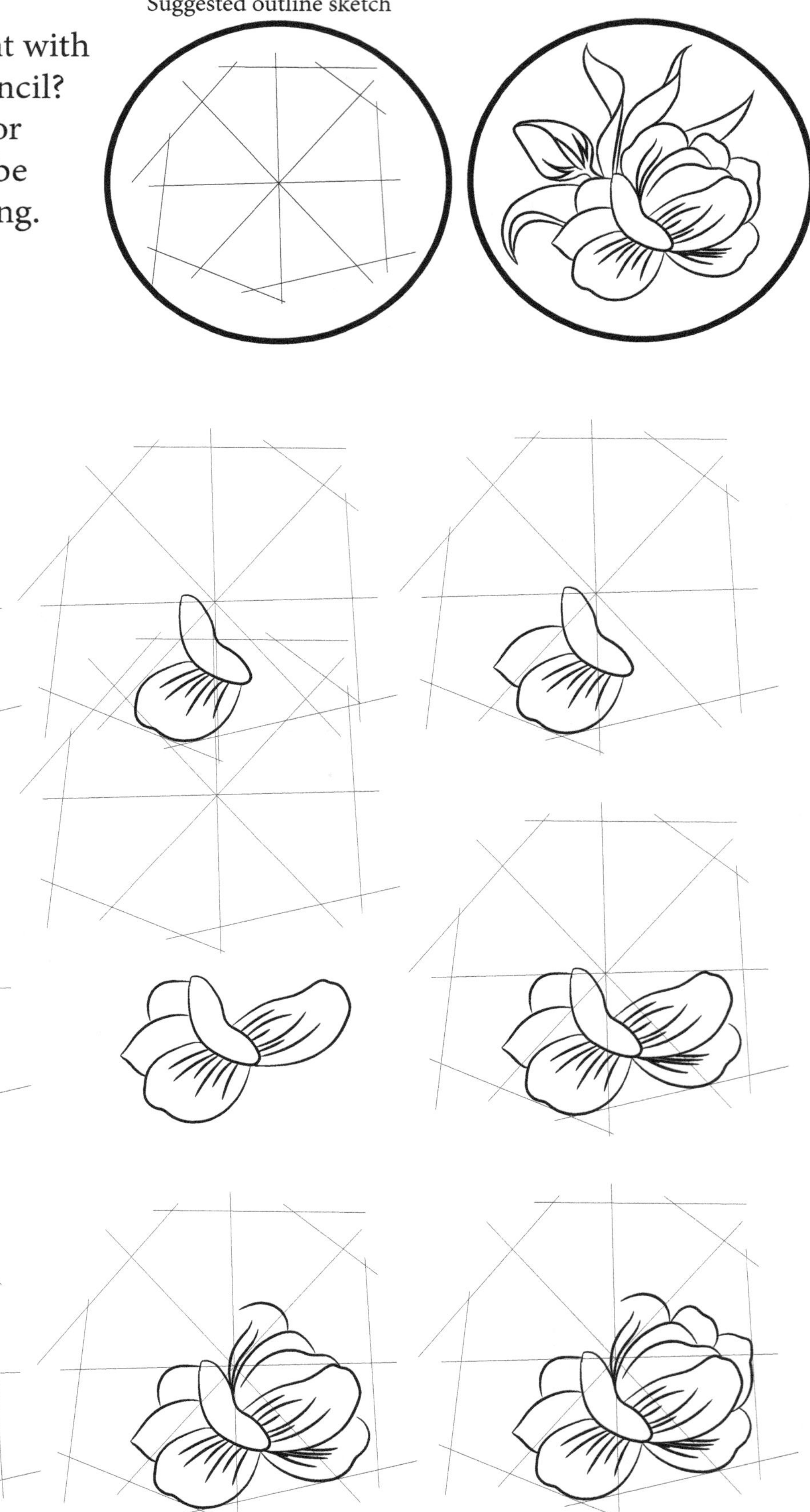

You can download blank grids to practice with in dark and light PDF formats by following the link below.

https://www.lipdf.com/product/grids/

https://www.lipdf.com/product/htdbooks/
Password: 6t5we3

10. Patience is key. If you
are getting irritated with
your work, leave it for now
and come back to it later.

Suggested outline sketch

You can download blank grids to practice with in dark and light PDF formats by following the link below.

https://www.lipdf.com/product/grids/

11. You could have a go at very roughly sketching out the shapes, then going over the lines in pen. Once finished, erase out the rough lines.

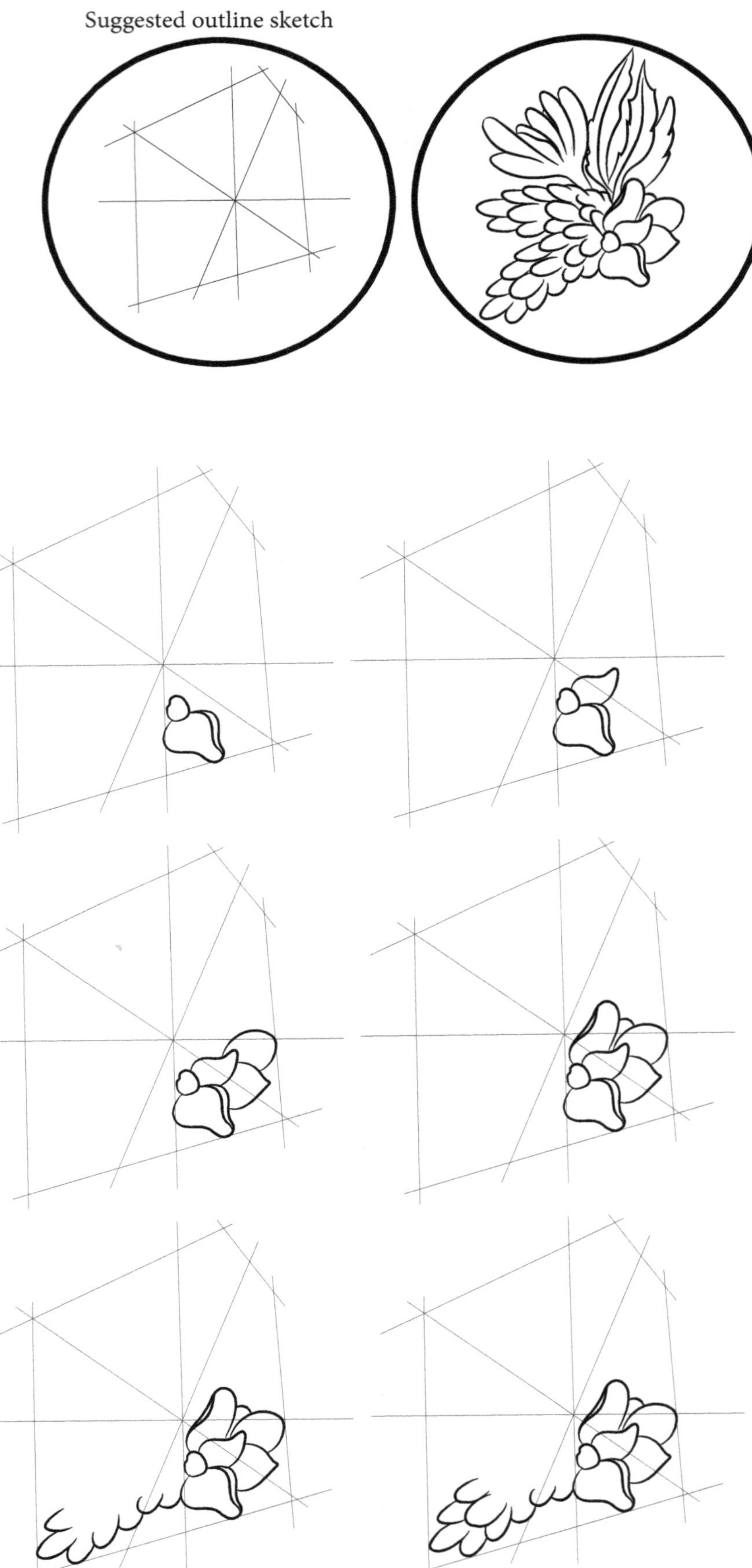

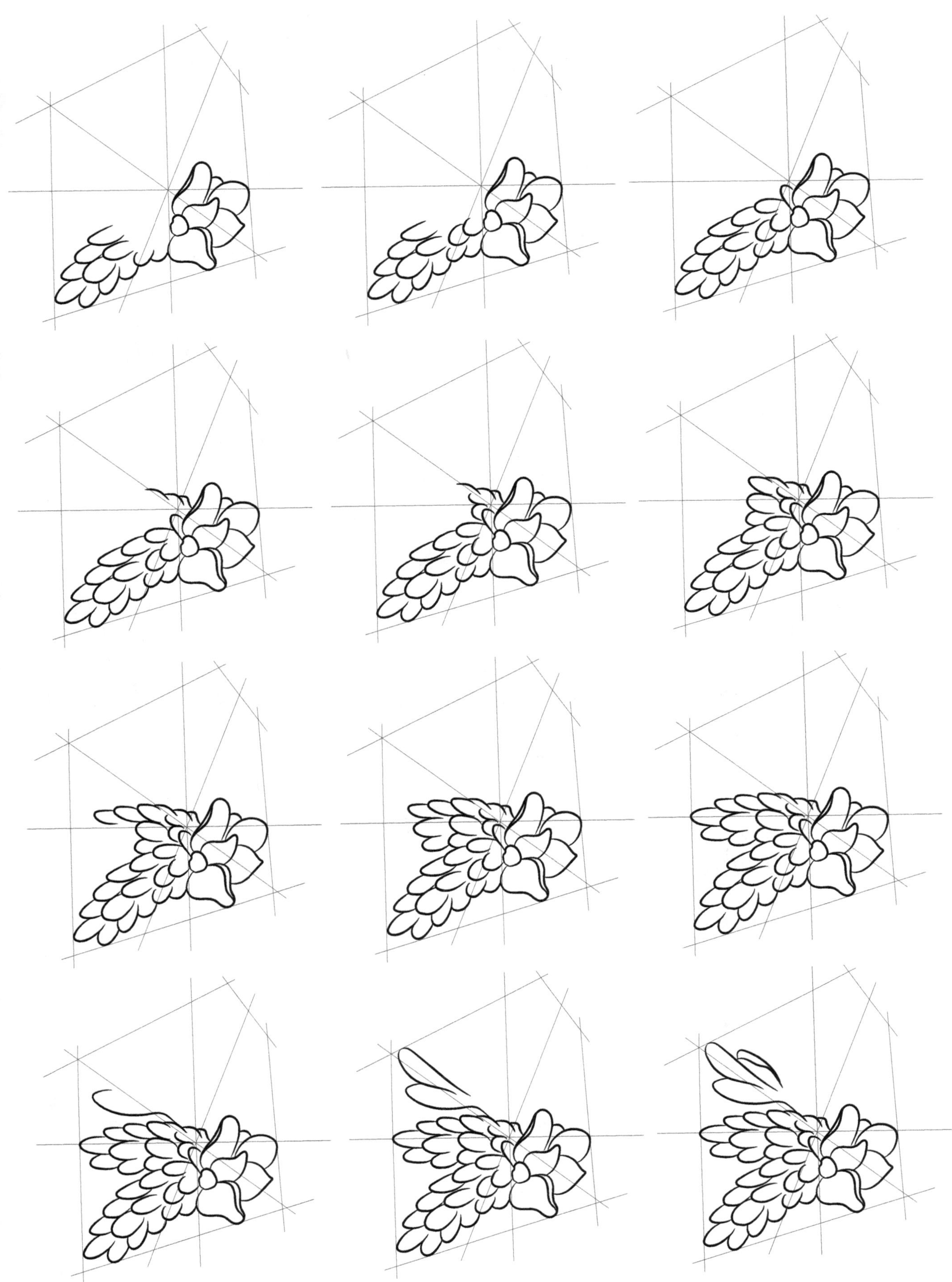

You can download blank grids to practice with in dark and light PDF formats by following the link below.

https://www.lipdf.com/product/grids/

12. If you struggle with this particular drawing, stop where you are and try another page in this book. You can always come back to this page later.

Suggested outline sketch

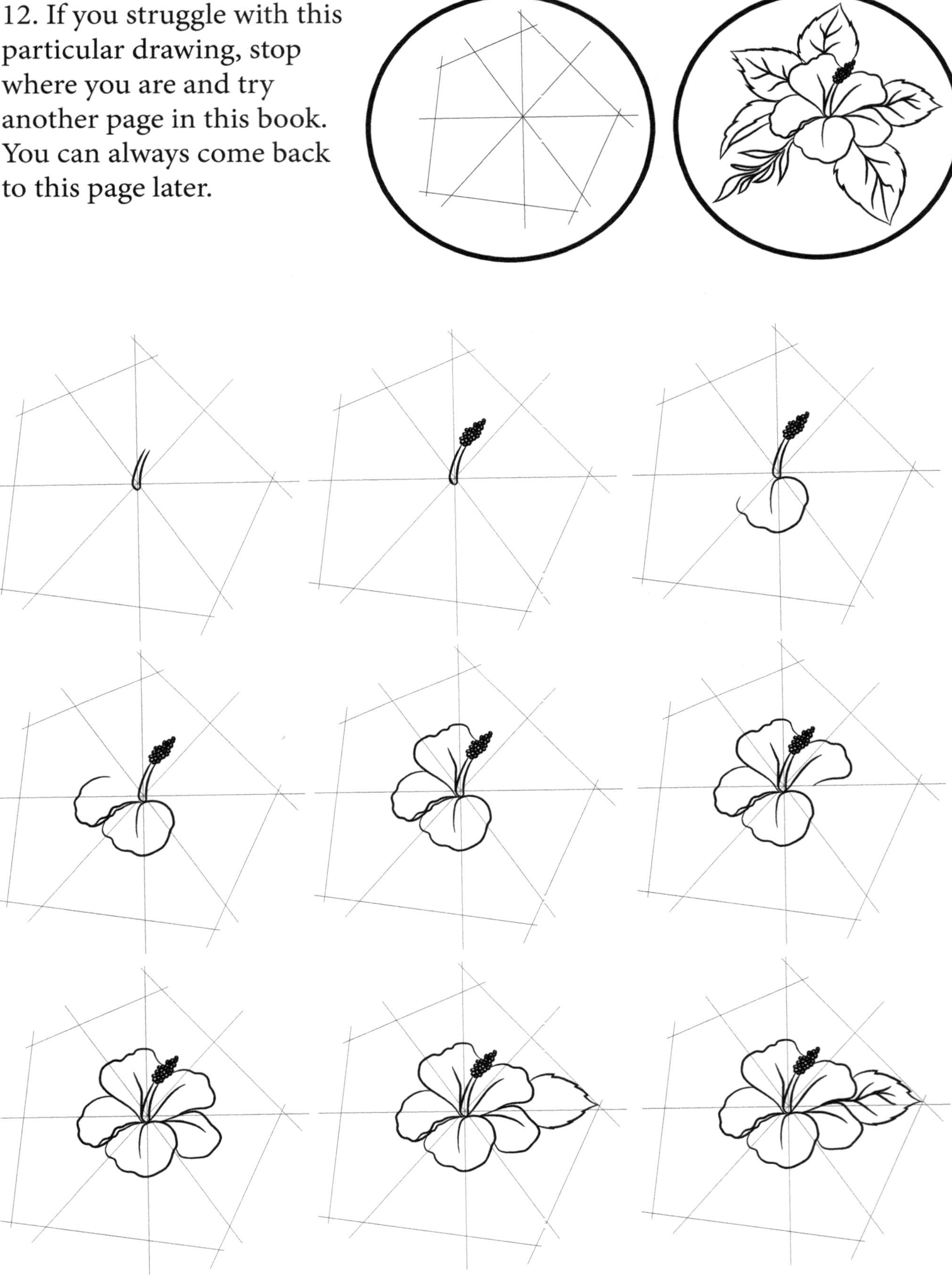

	A	B	C	D	E	F	G	H
1								
2								
3								
4								
5								
6								
7								
8								
9								
10								
11								
12								

13. Drawing a little everyday will help your drawing improve, stick with it!

Suggested outline sketch

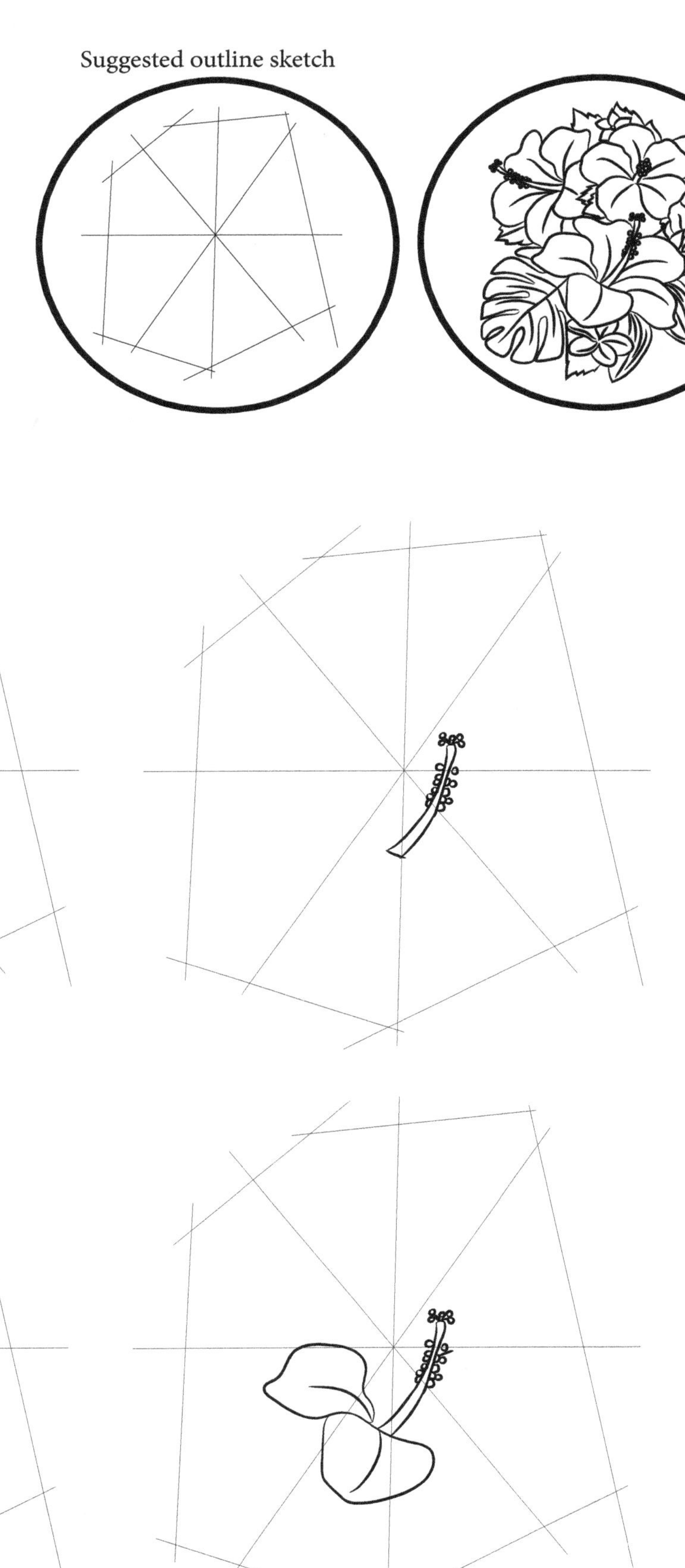

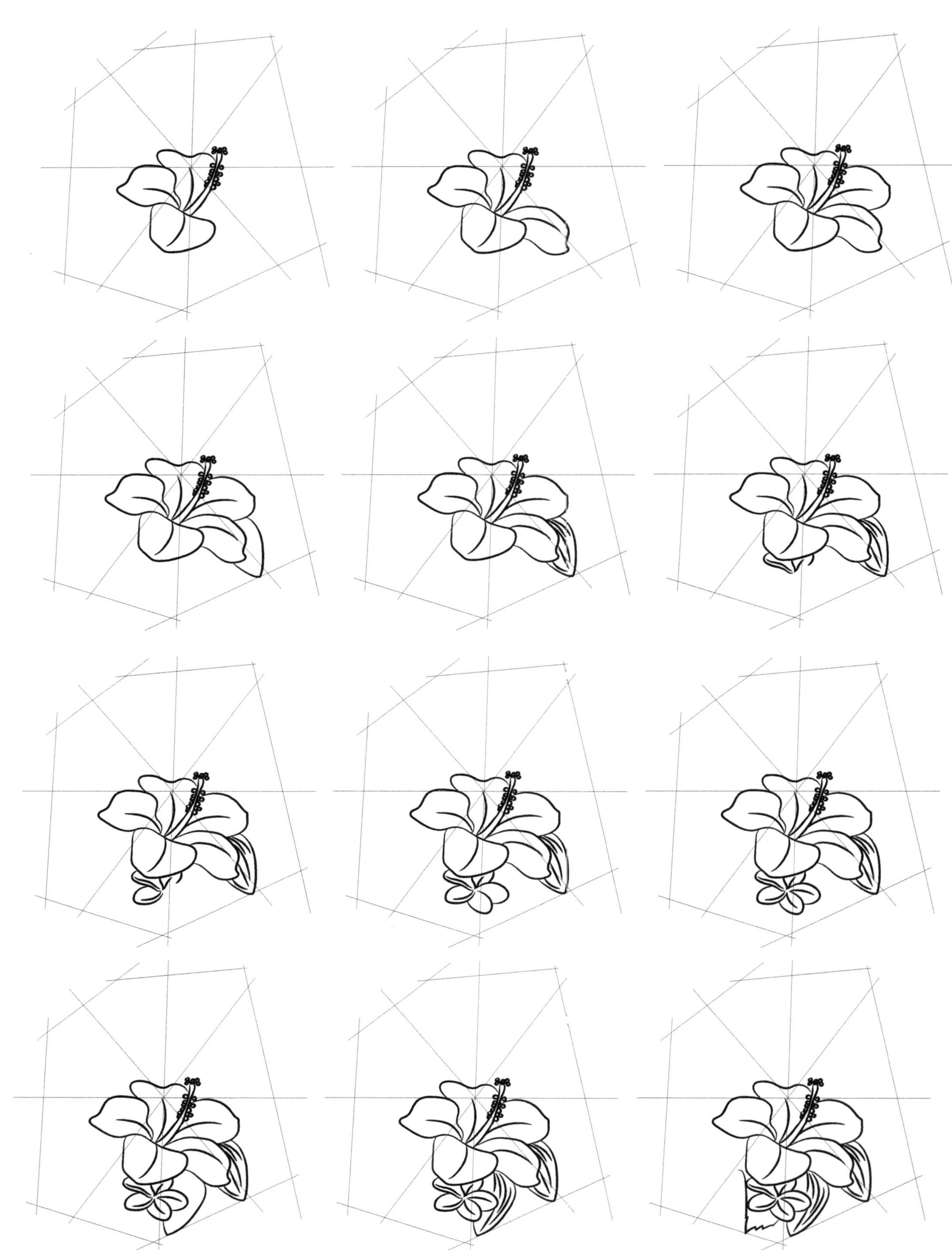

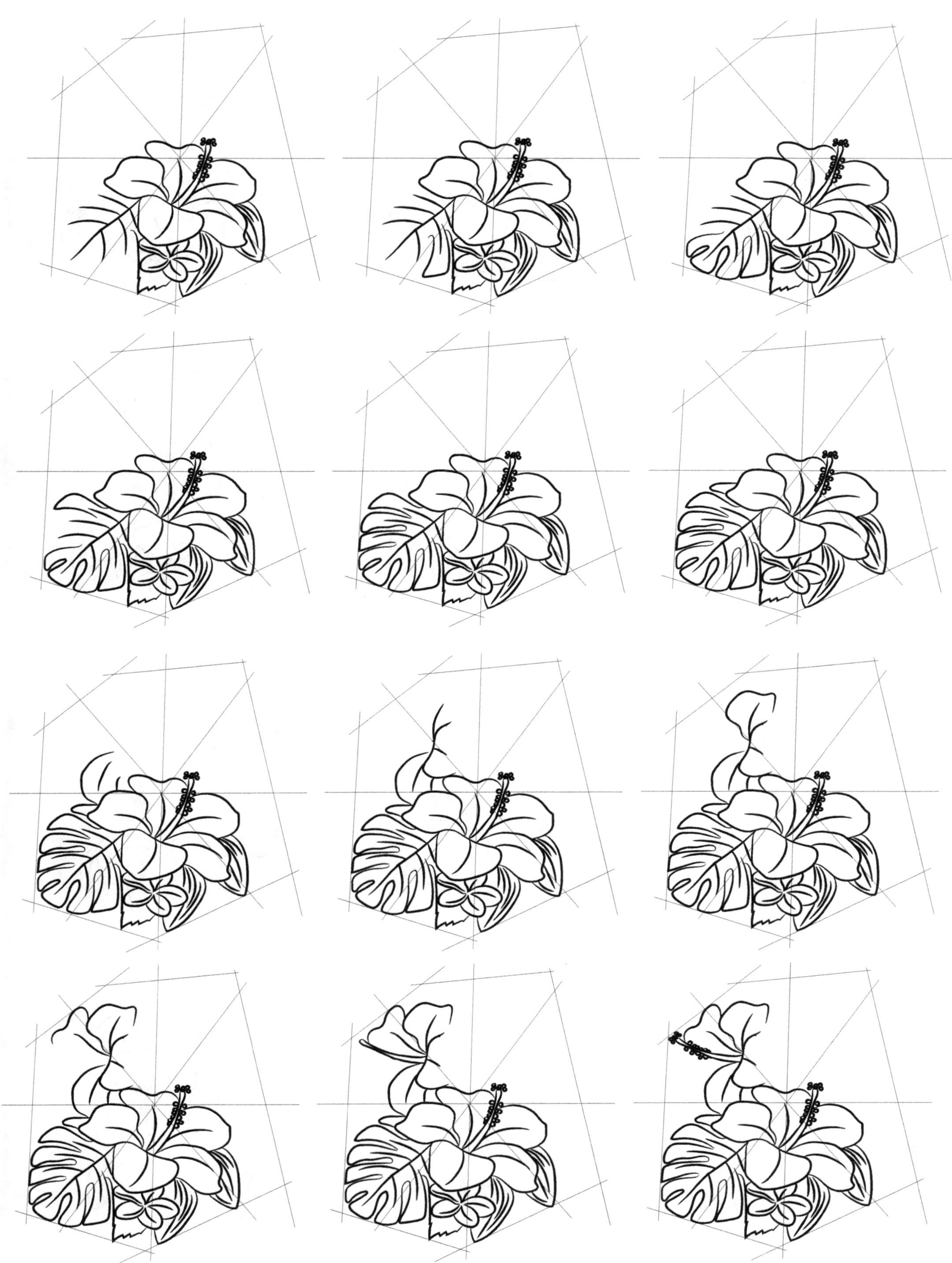

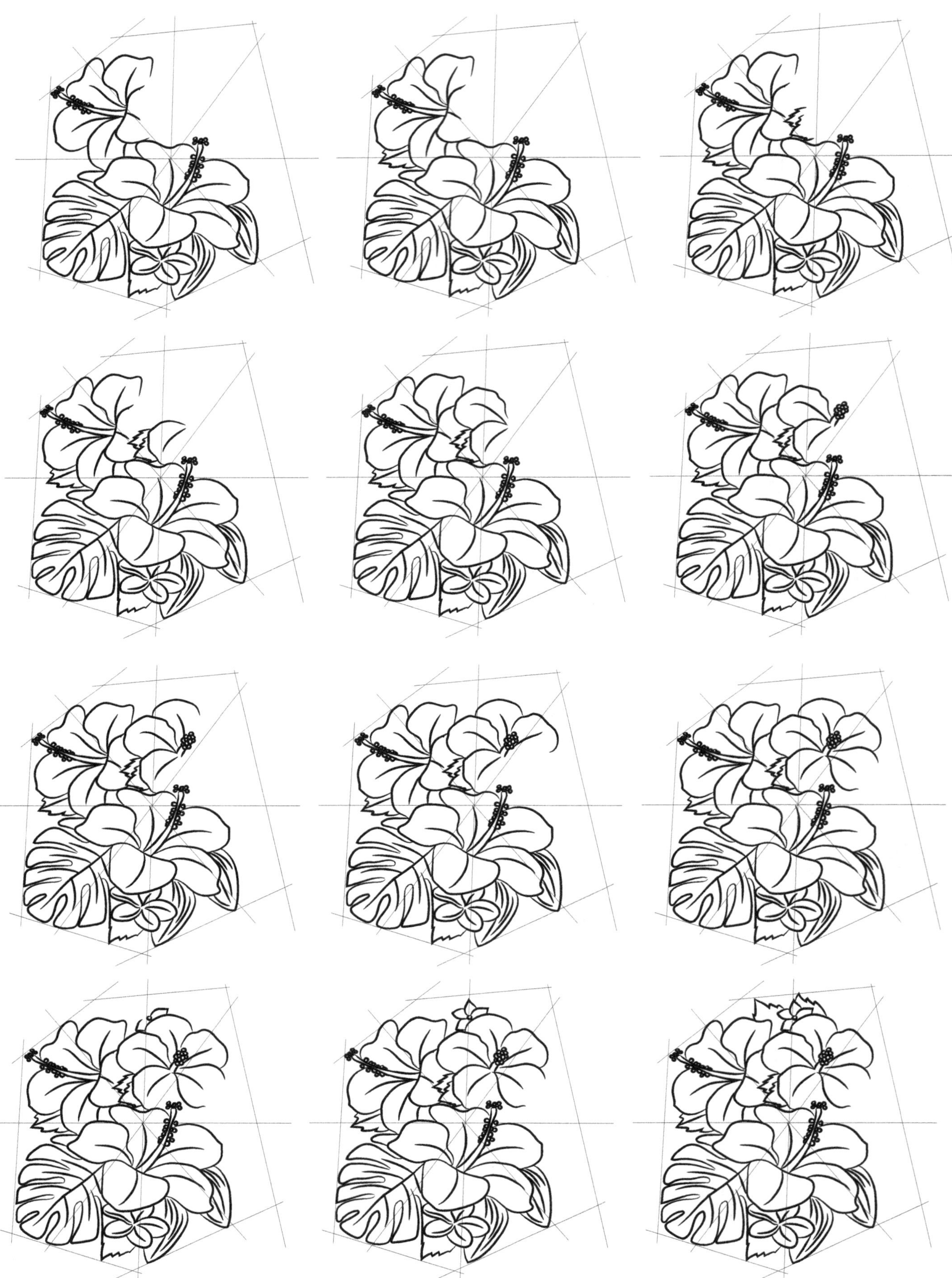

You can download blank grids to practice with in dark and light PDF formats by following the link below.

https://www.lipdf.com/product/grids/

14. The first stroke of your pencil can often be the most daunting but give it a go and see where the drawing takes you!

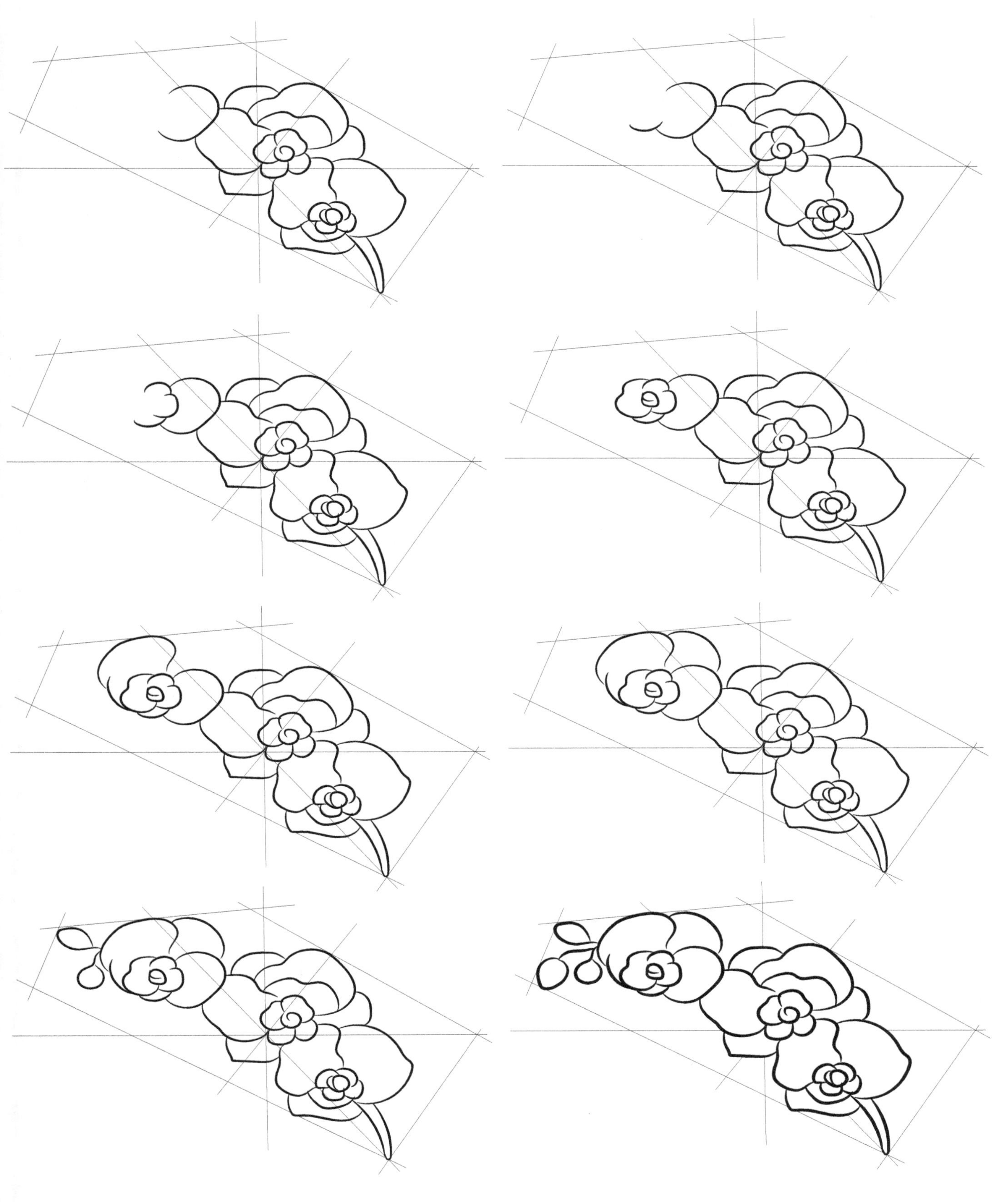

You can download blank grids to practice with in dark and light PDF formats by following the link below.

https://www.lipdf.com/product/grids/

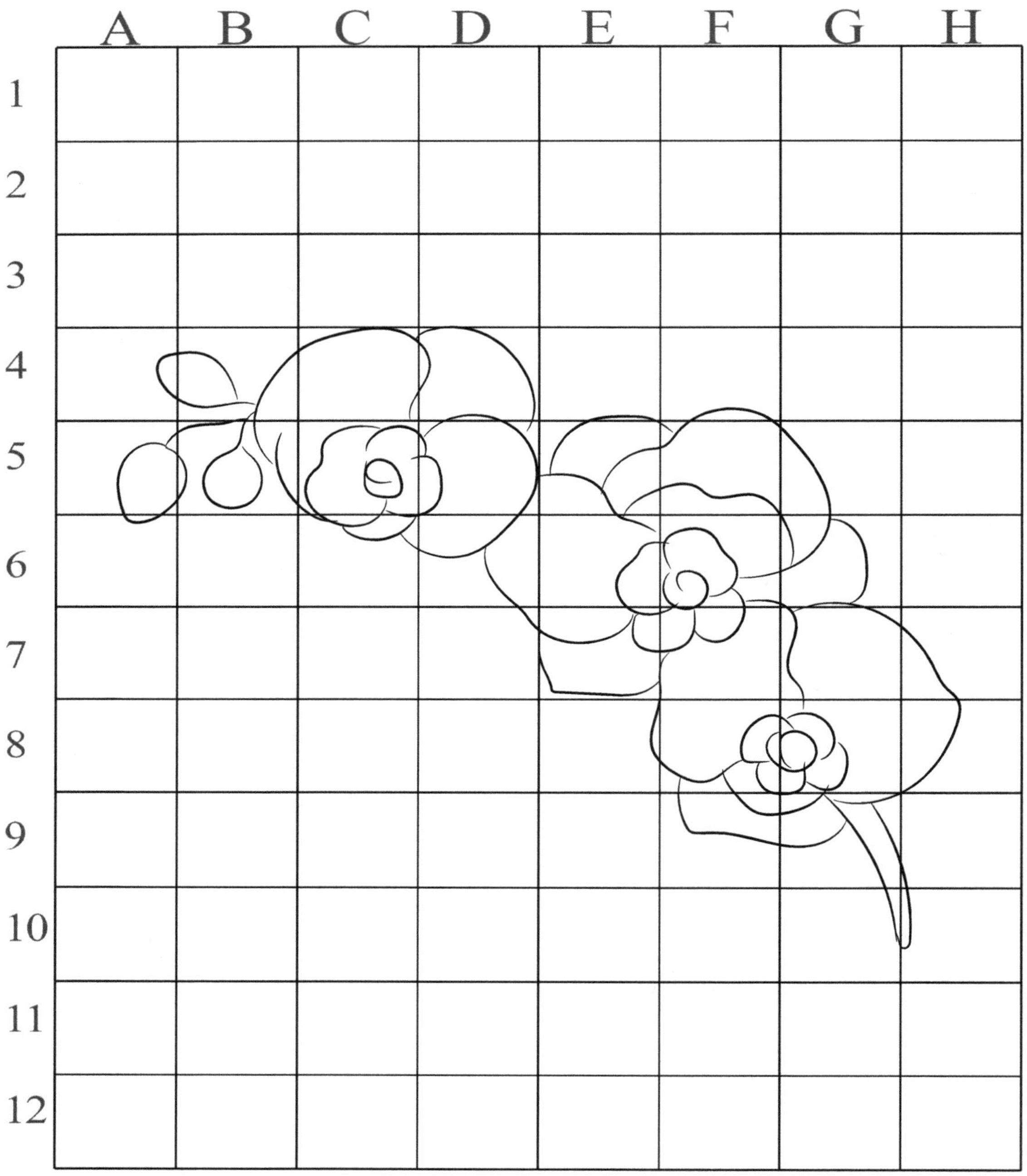

15. If you want to, you
could practice different
types of pencil strokes
on a scrap piece of
paper. What happens
when you press hard
with the pencil? What
happens when you use
the edge of the pencil
rather than the point?

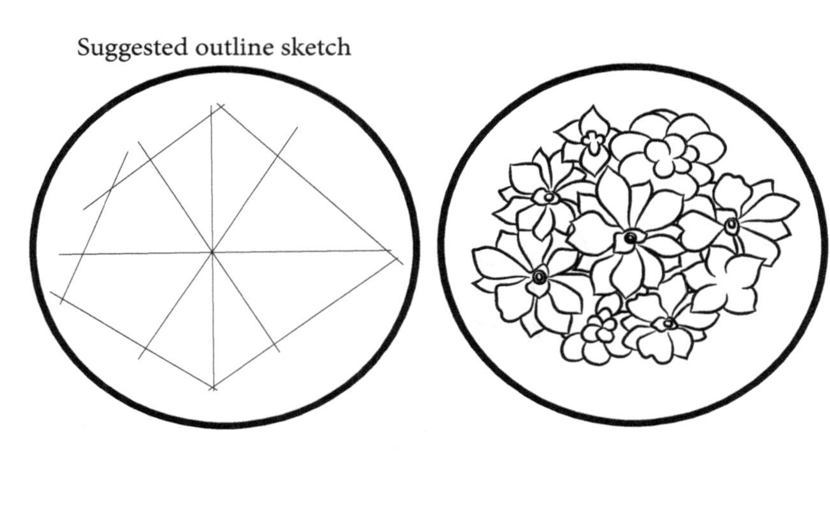
Suggested outline sketch

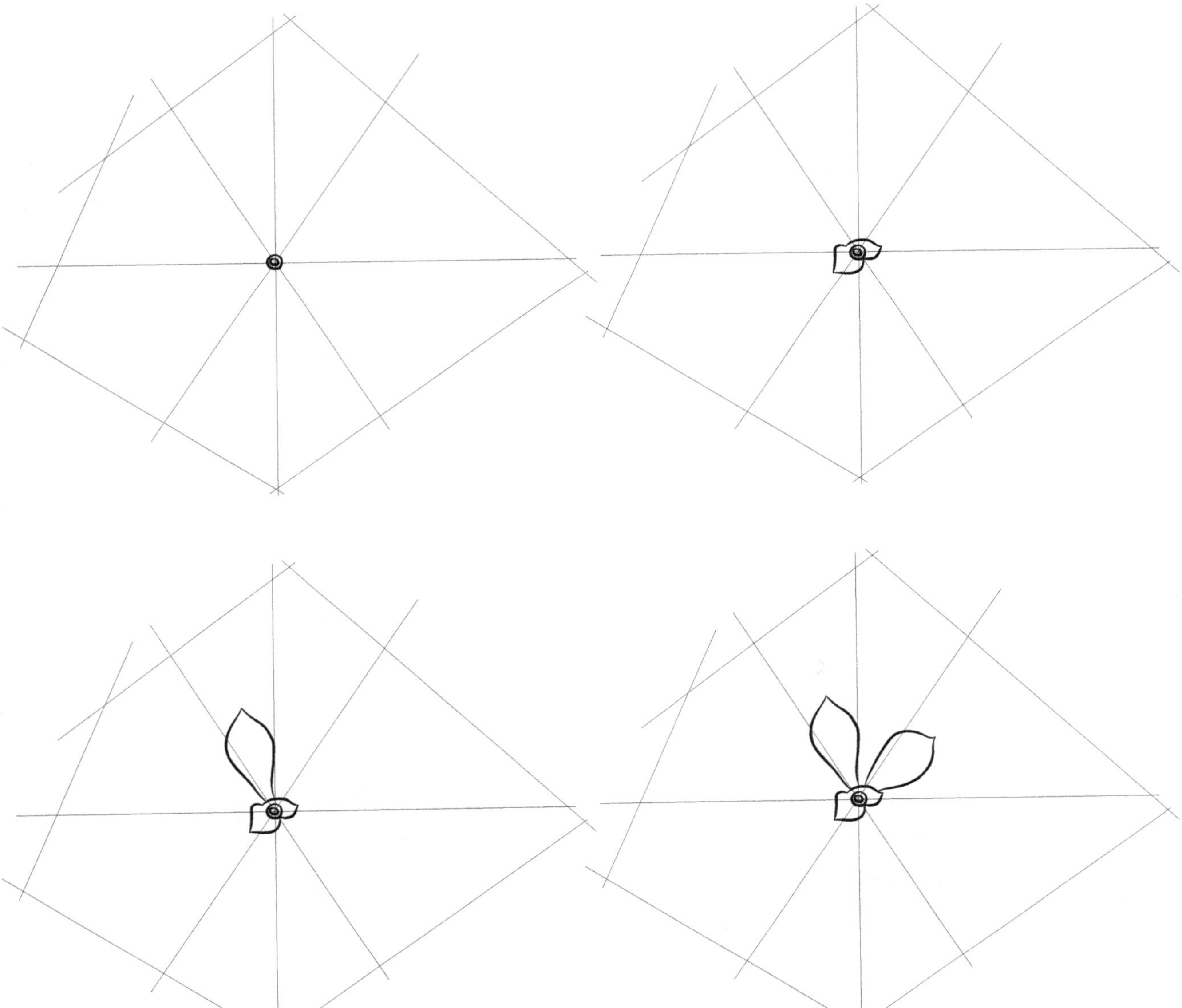

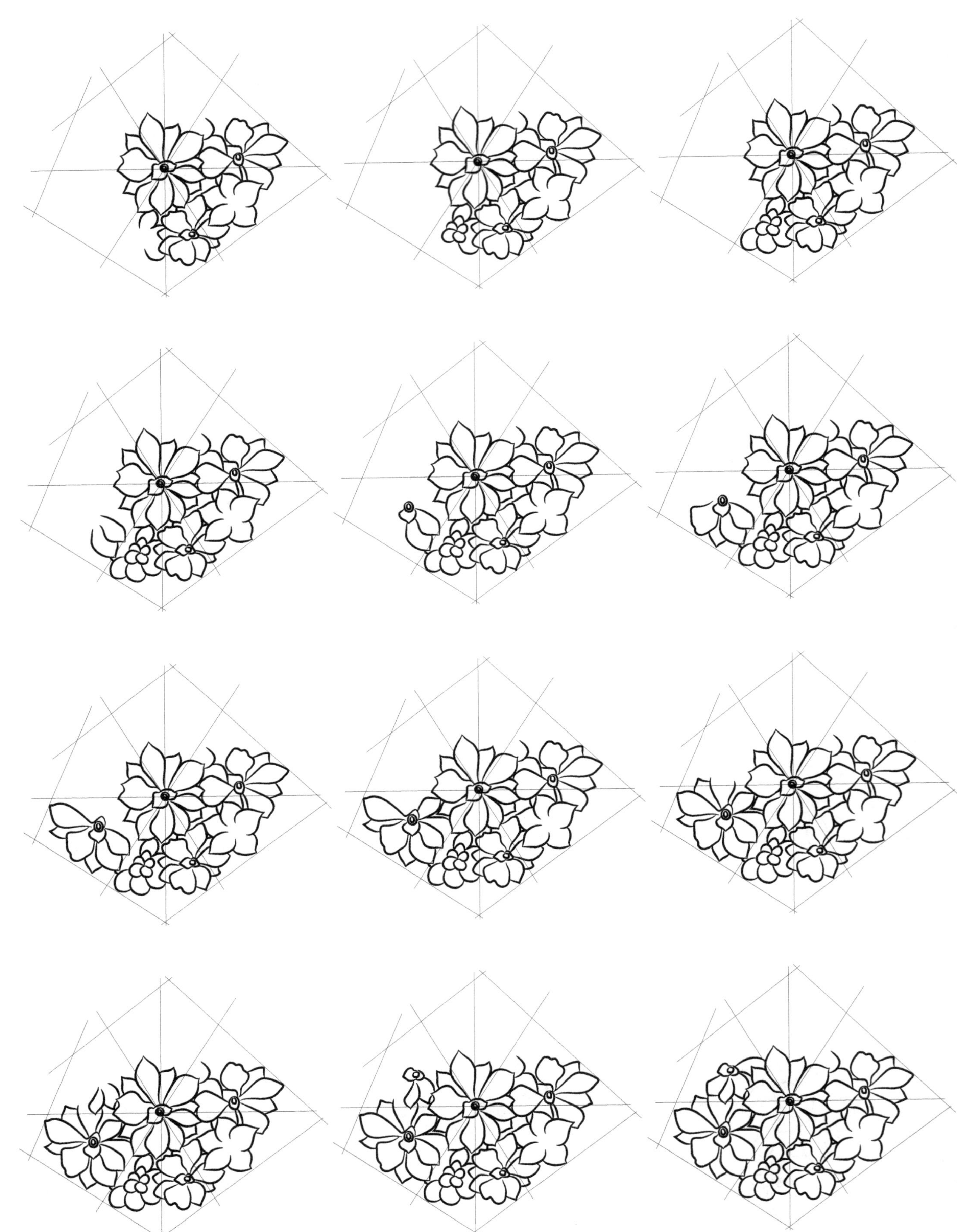

You can download blank grids to practice with in dark and light PDF formats by following the link below.

https://www.lipdf.com/product/grids/

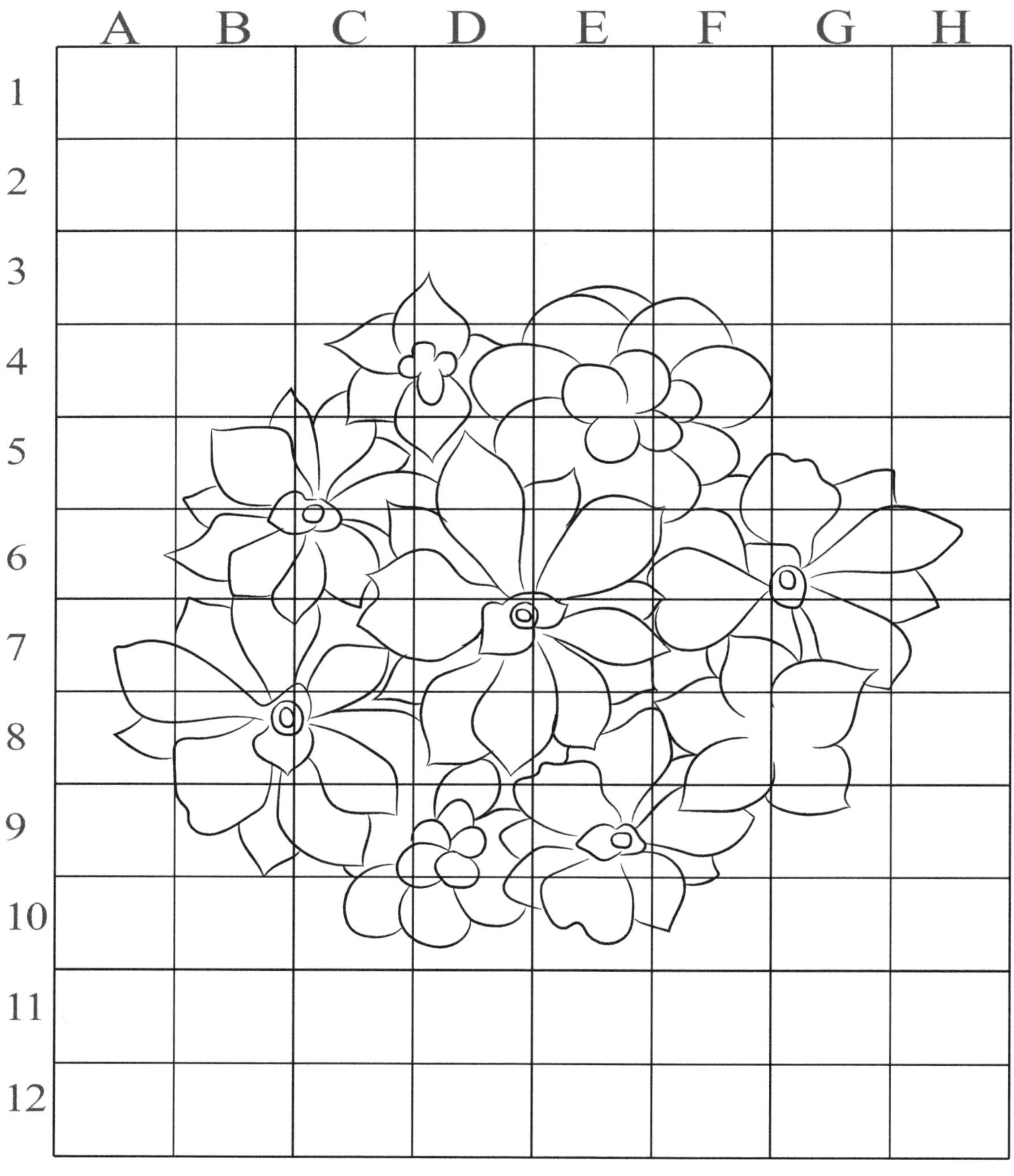

16. Always keep your hand relaxed, you will be surprised to see how your drawing flows on the paper when you aren't pressing too hard with the pencil.

Suggested outline sketch

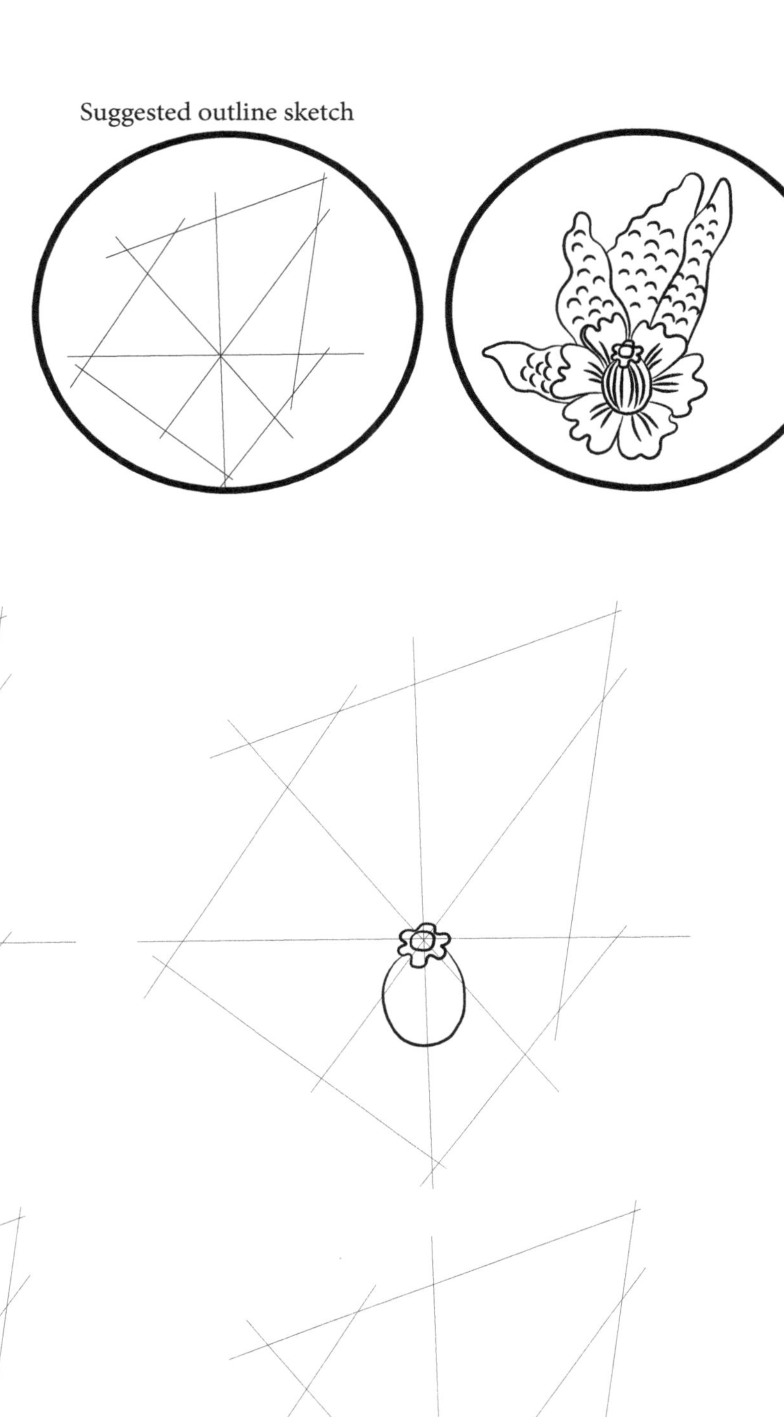

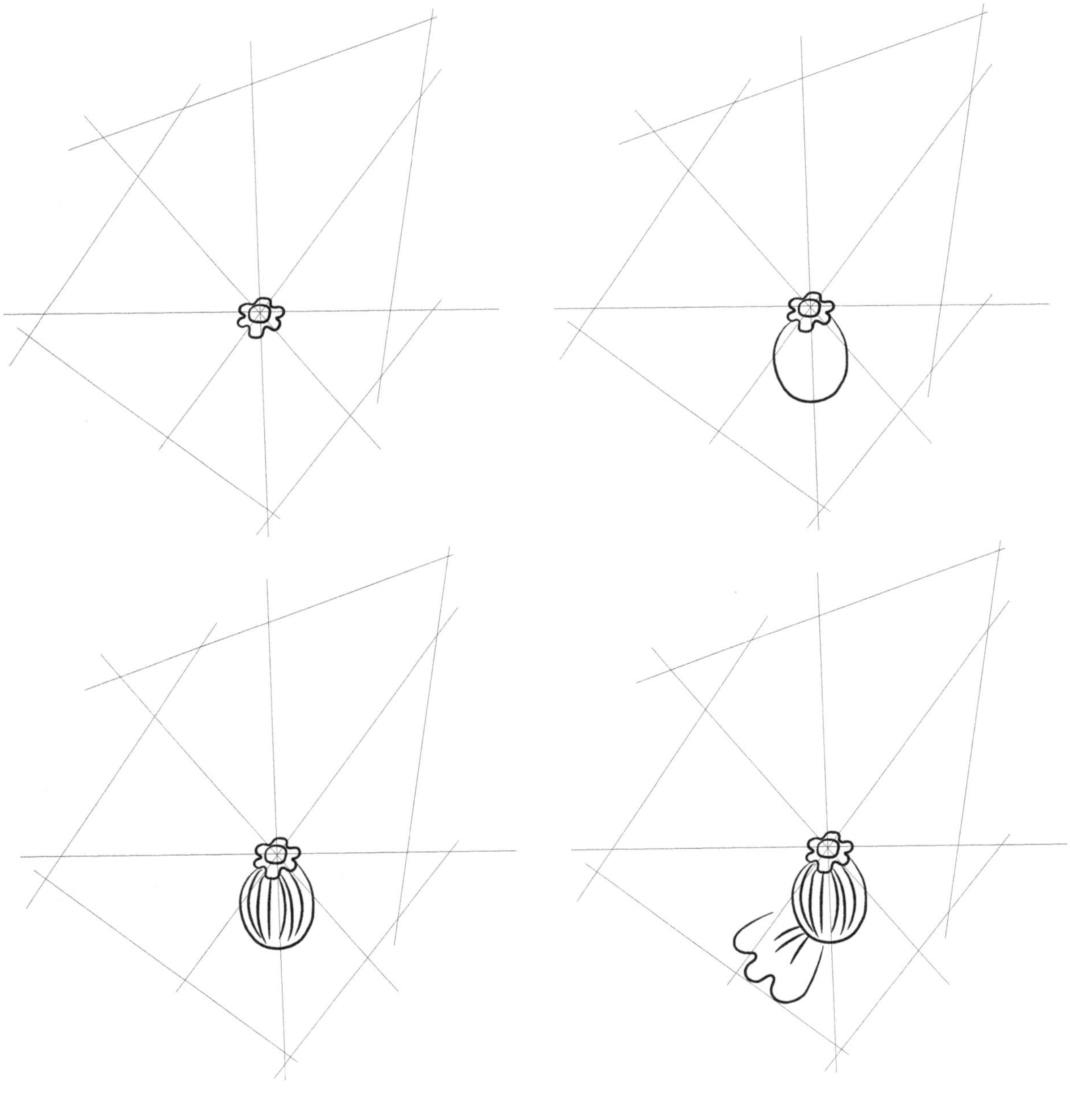

You can download blank grids to practice with in dark and light PDF formats by following the link below.

https://www.lipdf.com/product/grids/

17. Try out a "warm up" exercise before starting your drawing. Have a go at straight, curved and zig zag lines on a scrap piece of paper.

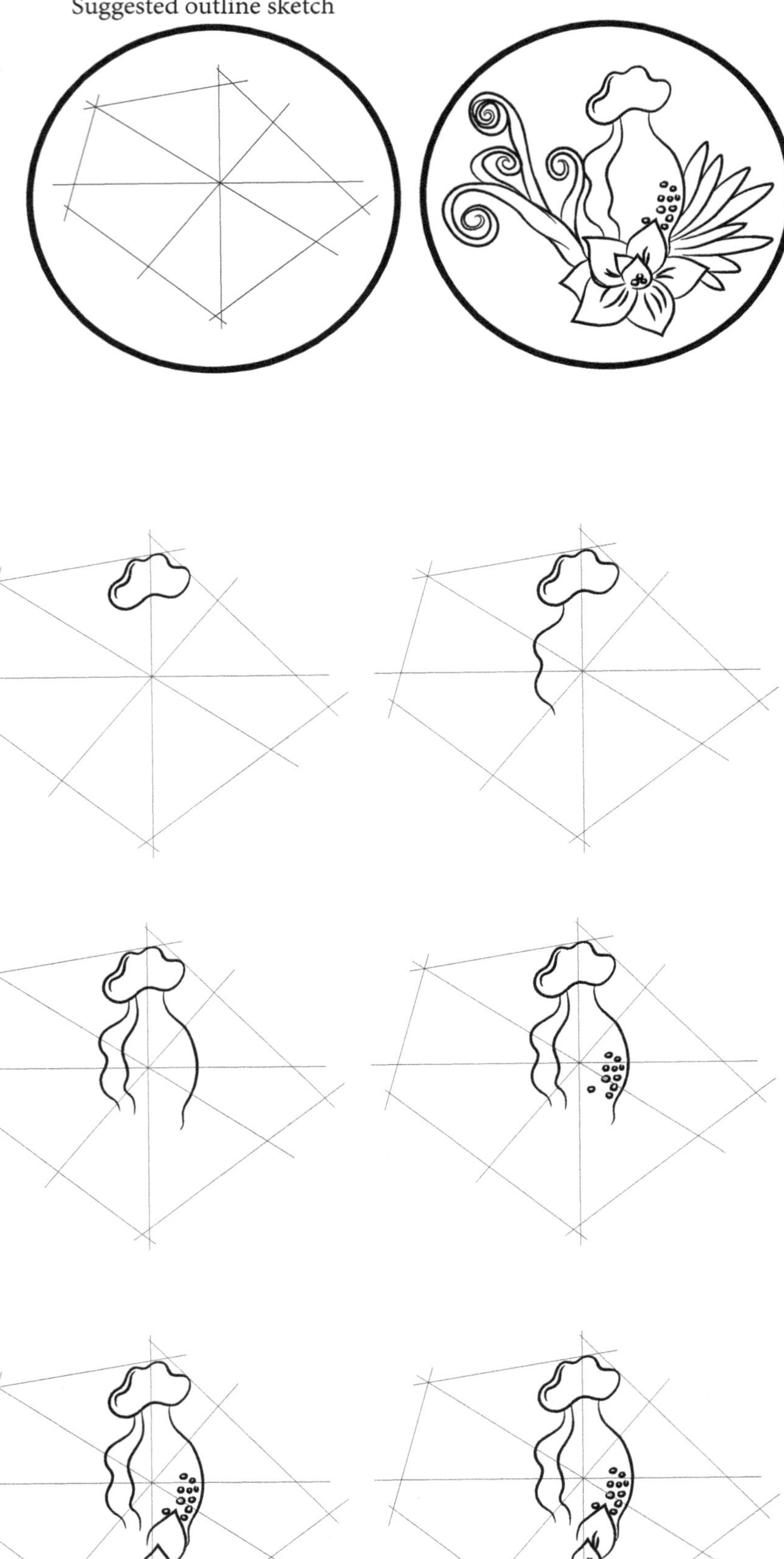

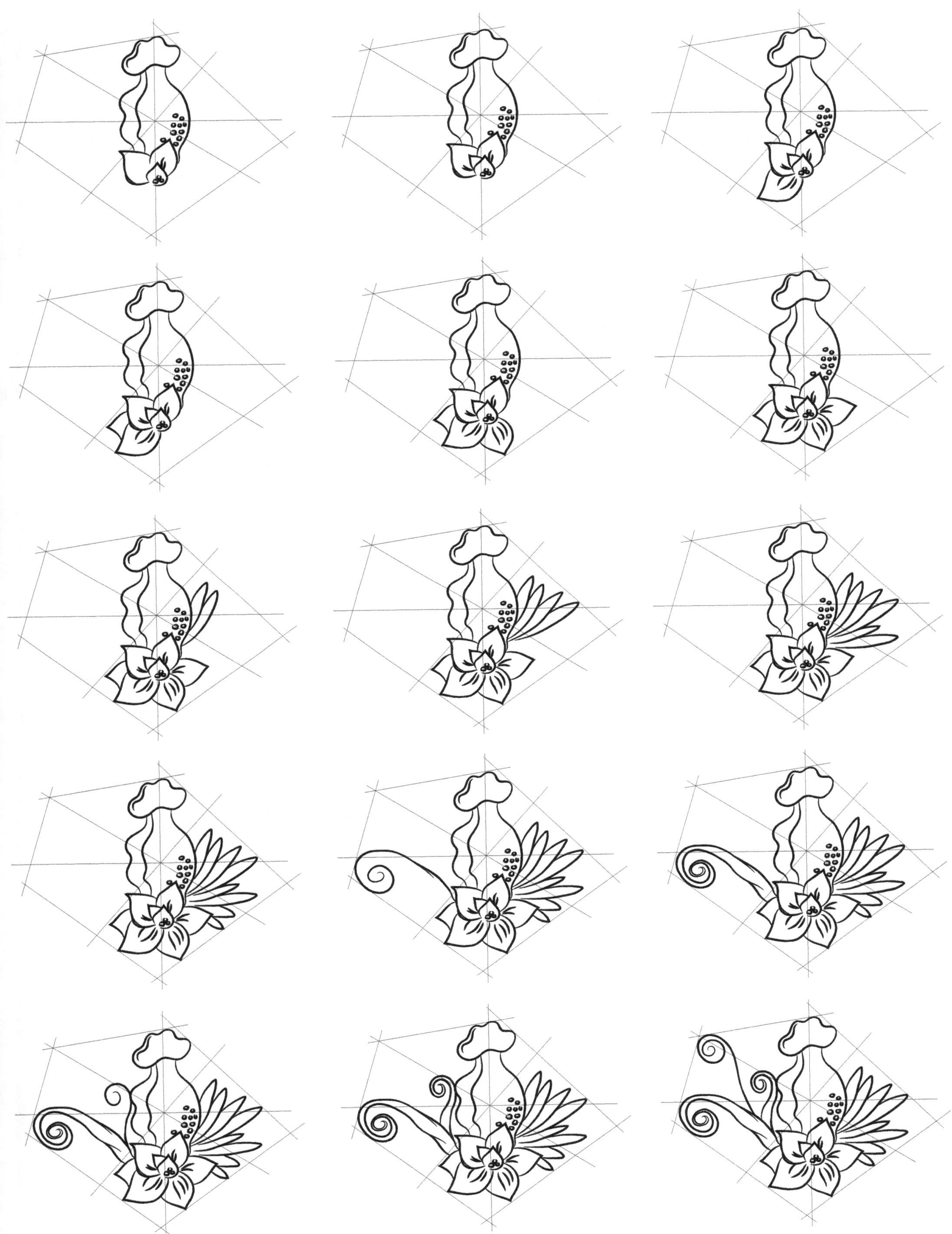

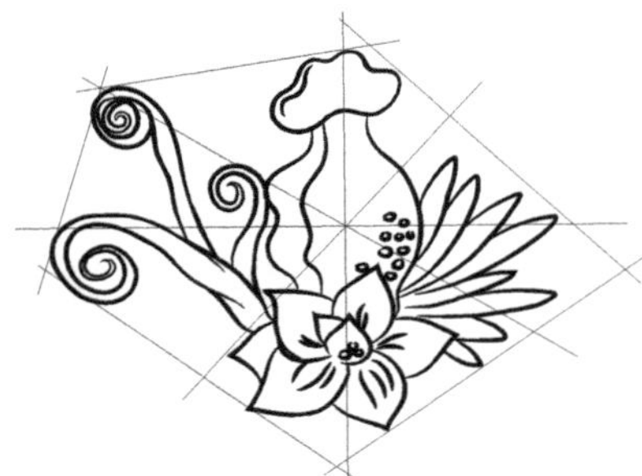

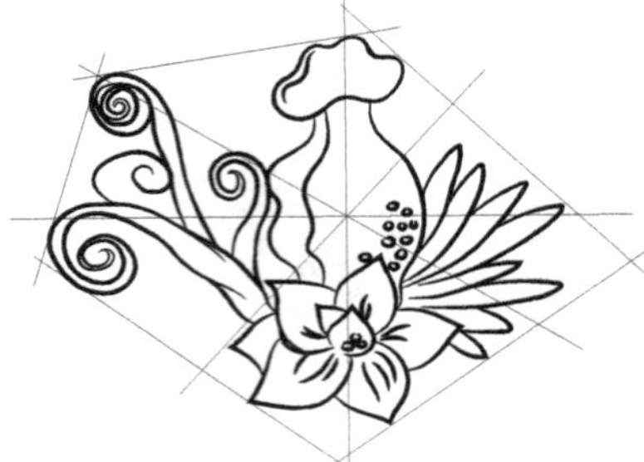

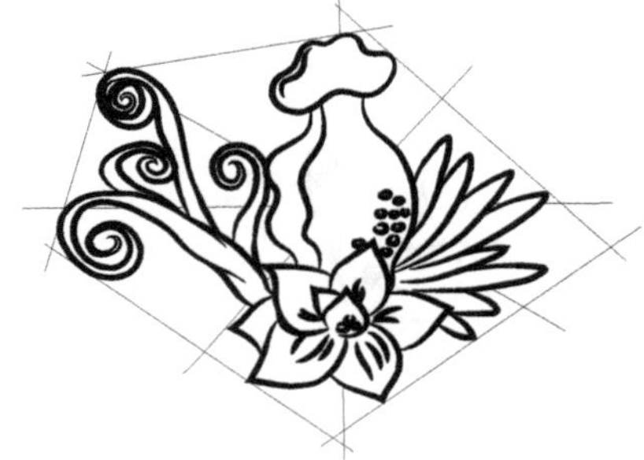

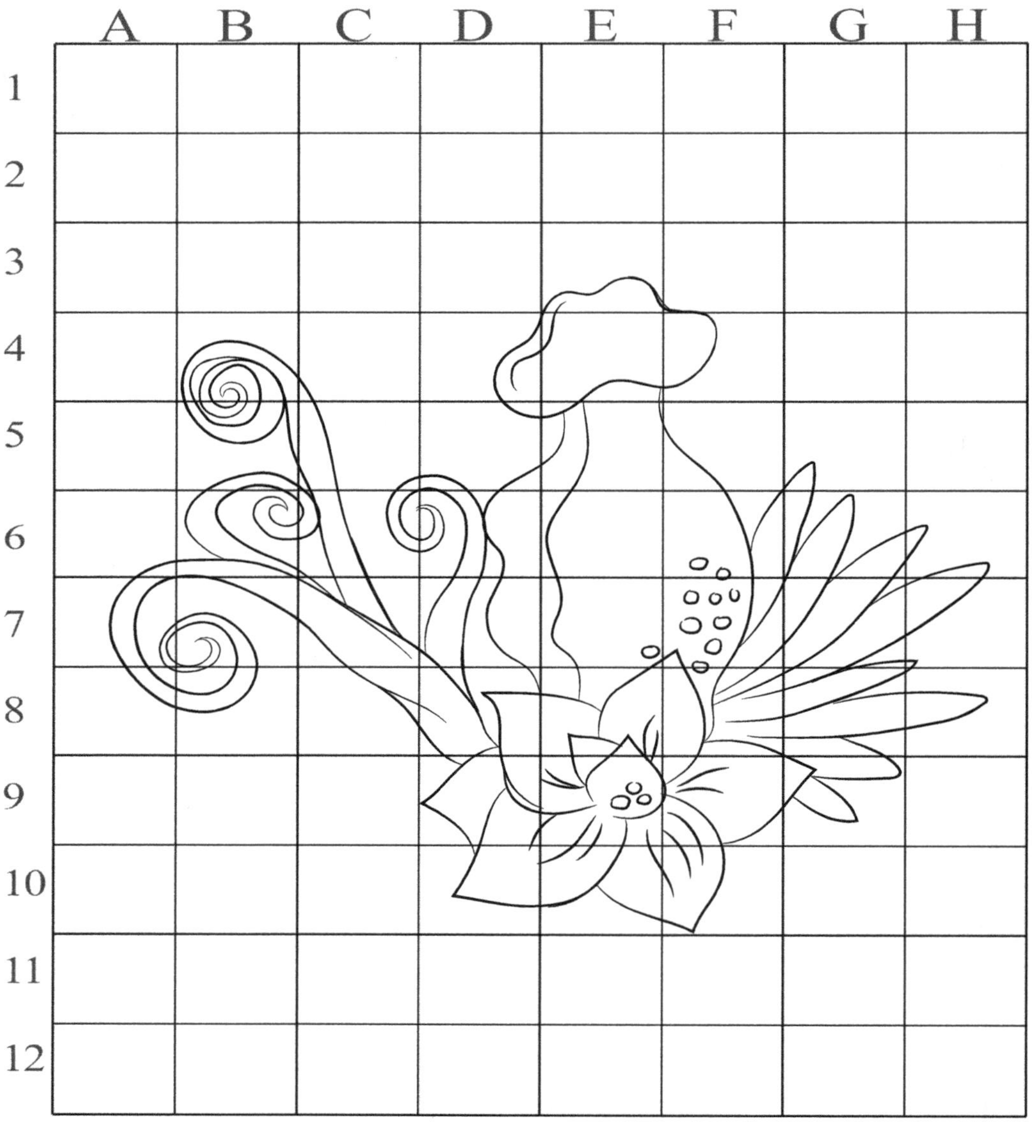
A B C D E F G H
1
2
3
4
5
6
7
8
9
10
11
12

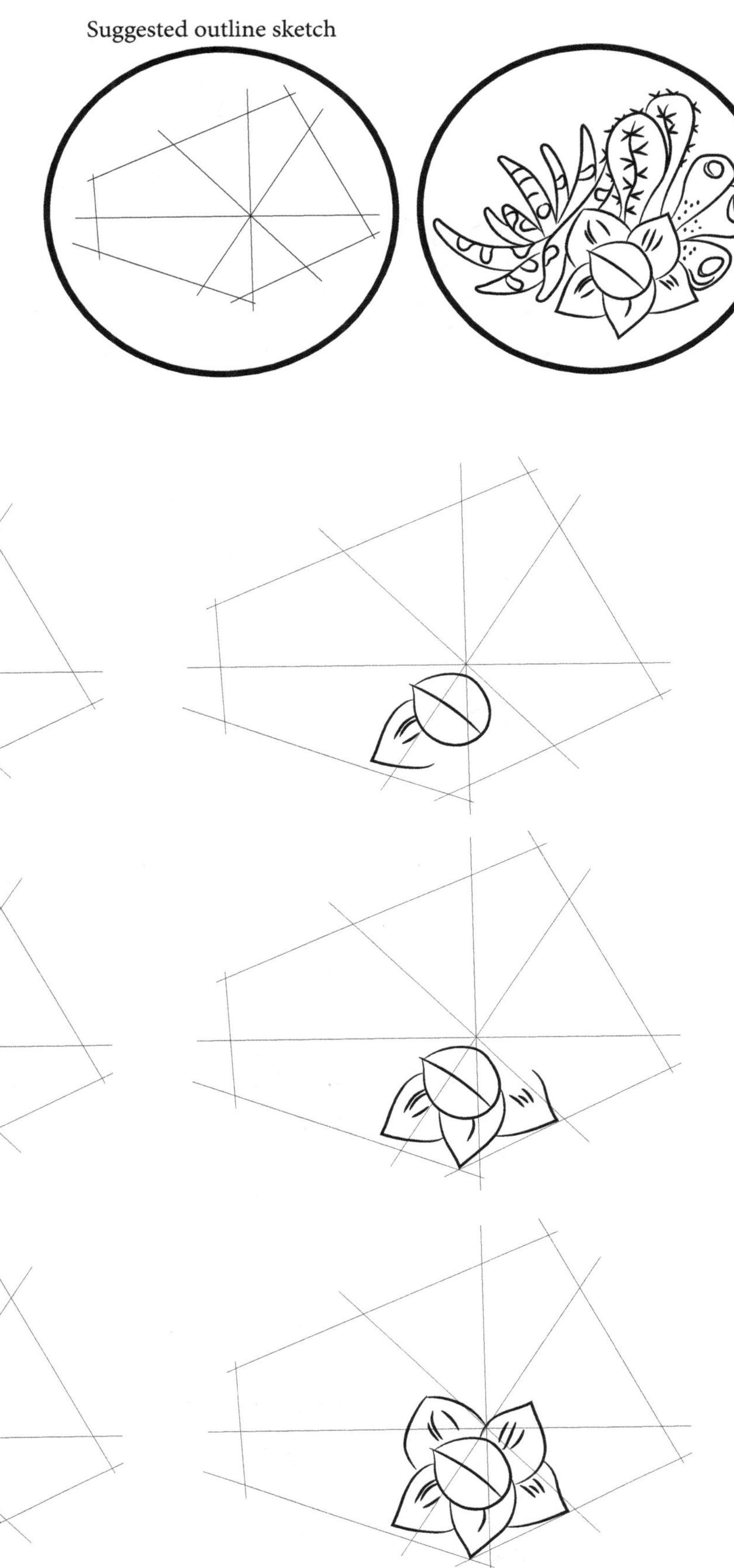

18. If you are struggling to draw a long line, try sketching much shorter lines joined together. You will find your pencil is much easier to control.

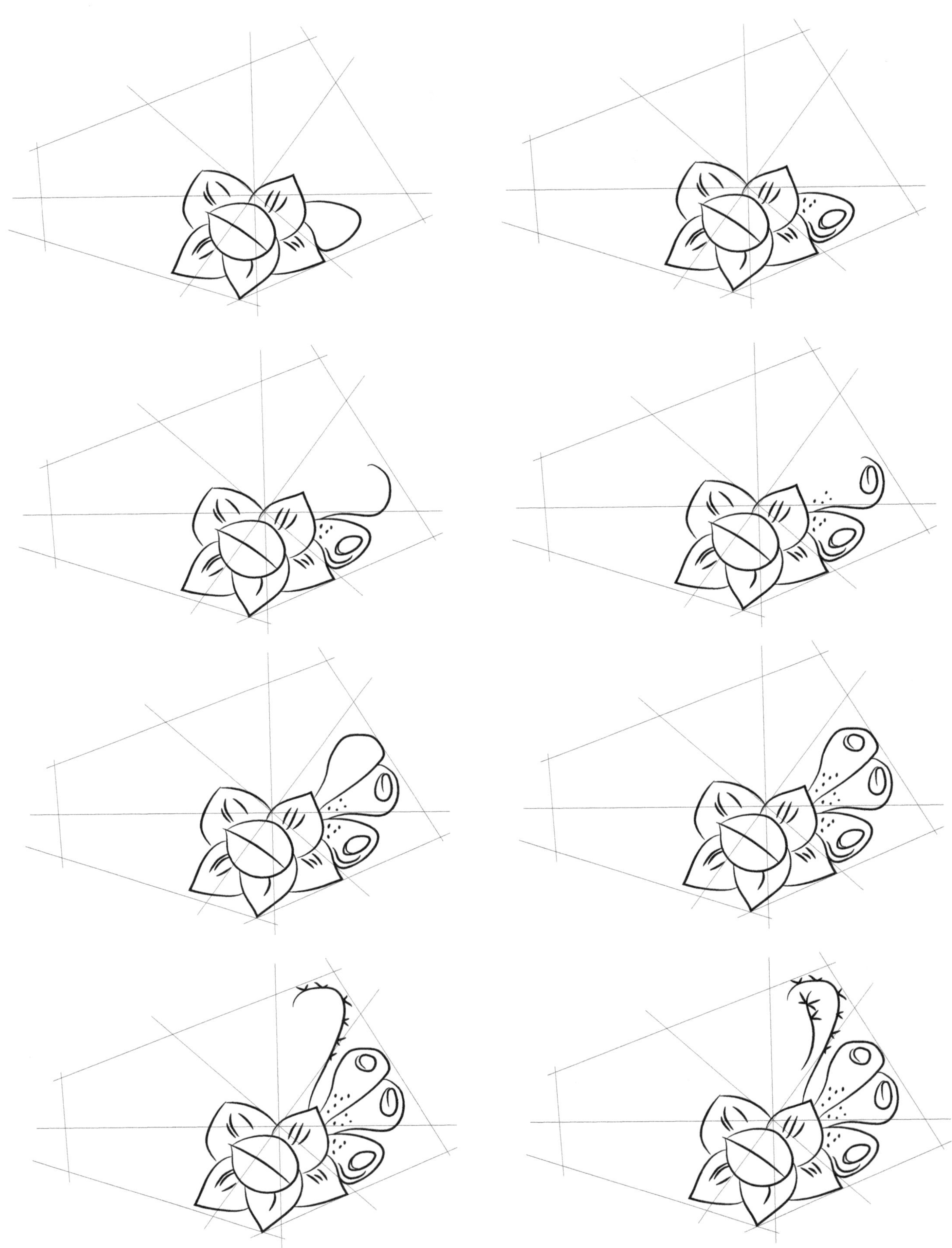

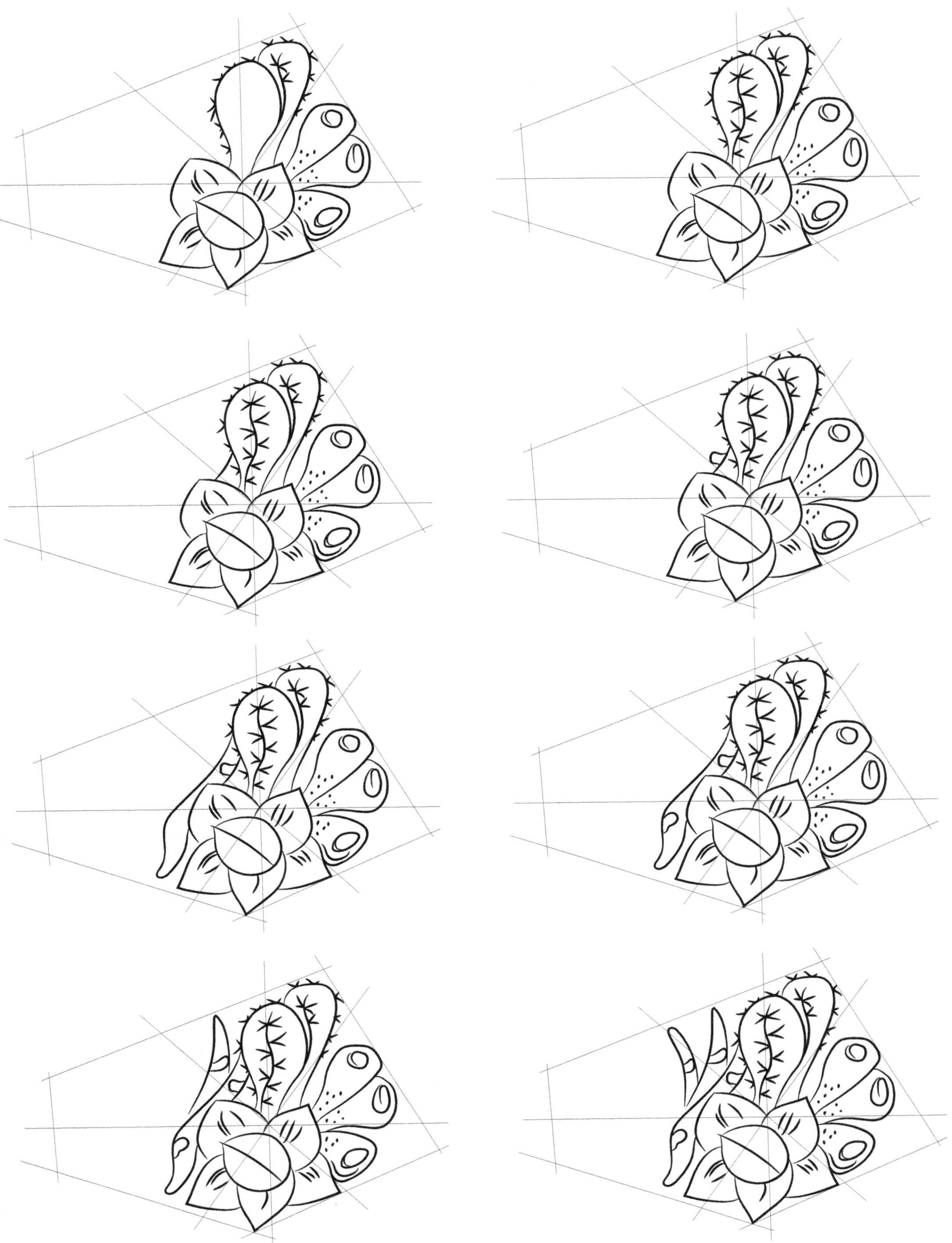

You can download blank grids to practice with in dark and light PDF formats by following the link below.

https://www.lipdf.com/product/grids/

19. Much like handwriting, everyone's drawing technique is unique, so don't feel disheartened if you draw differently to your friends and siblings – they probably feel the same way!

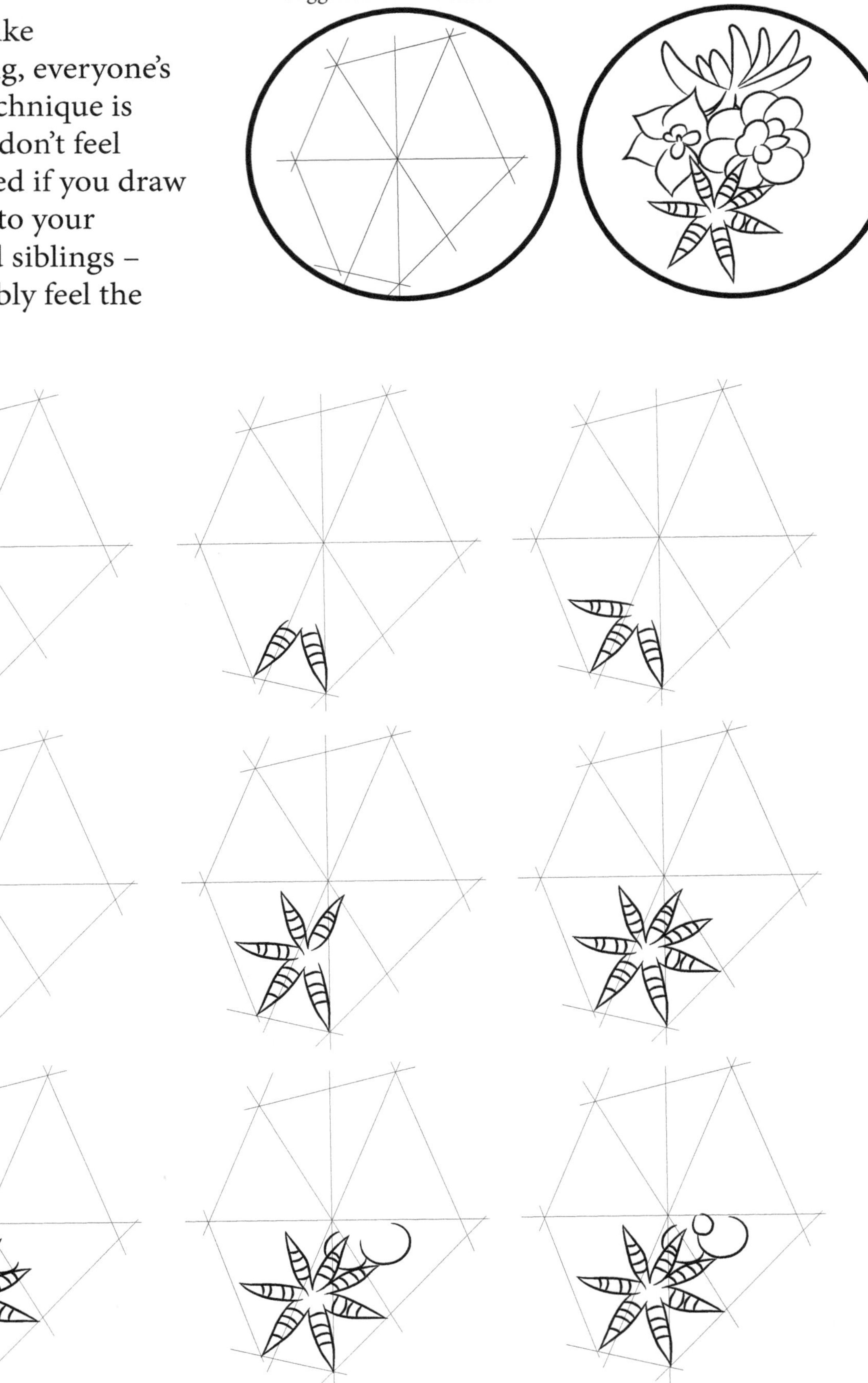

You can download blank grids to practice with in dark and light PDF formats by following the link below.

https://www.lipdf.com/product/grids/

20. Try not to get annoyed if what you've drawn on the paper isn't as you had envisioned, keep on going and you'll find that every pencil stroke will eventually come together.

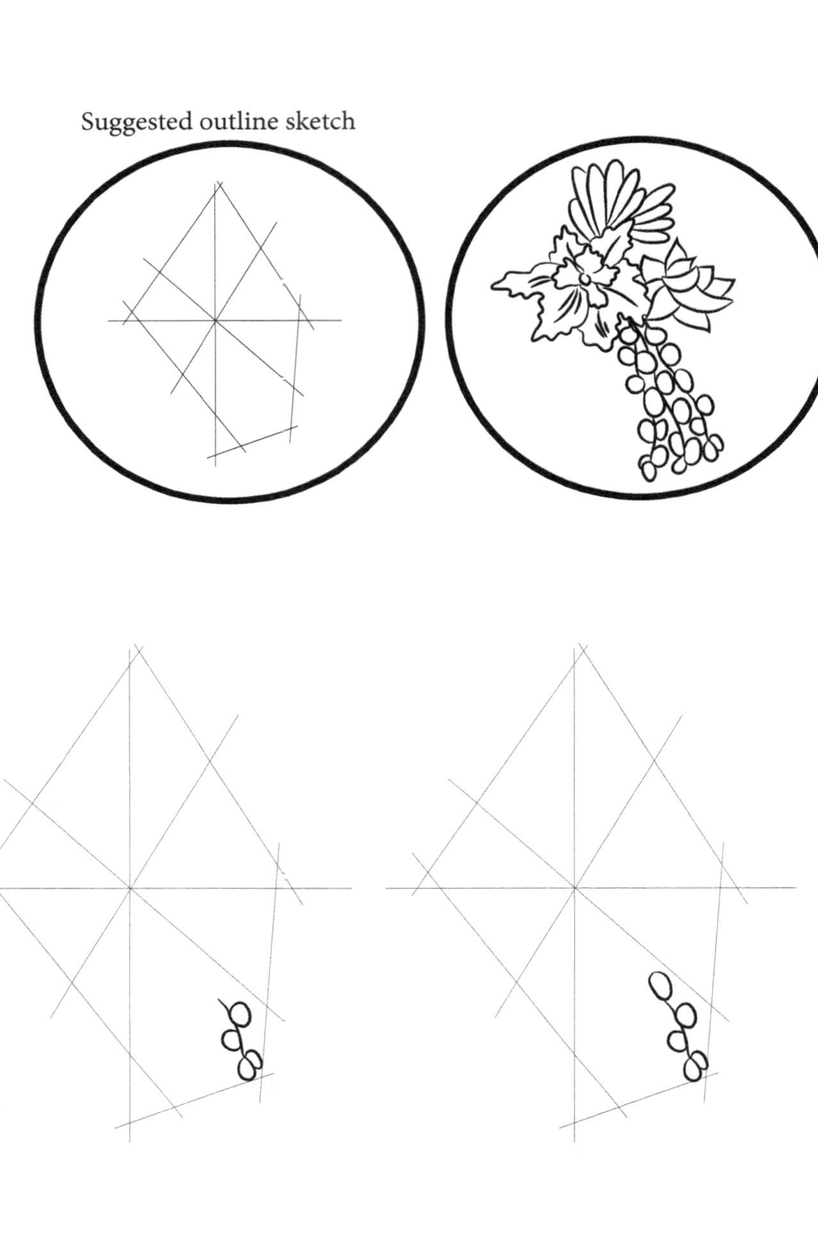
Suggested outline sketch

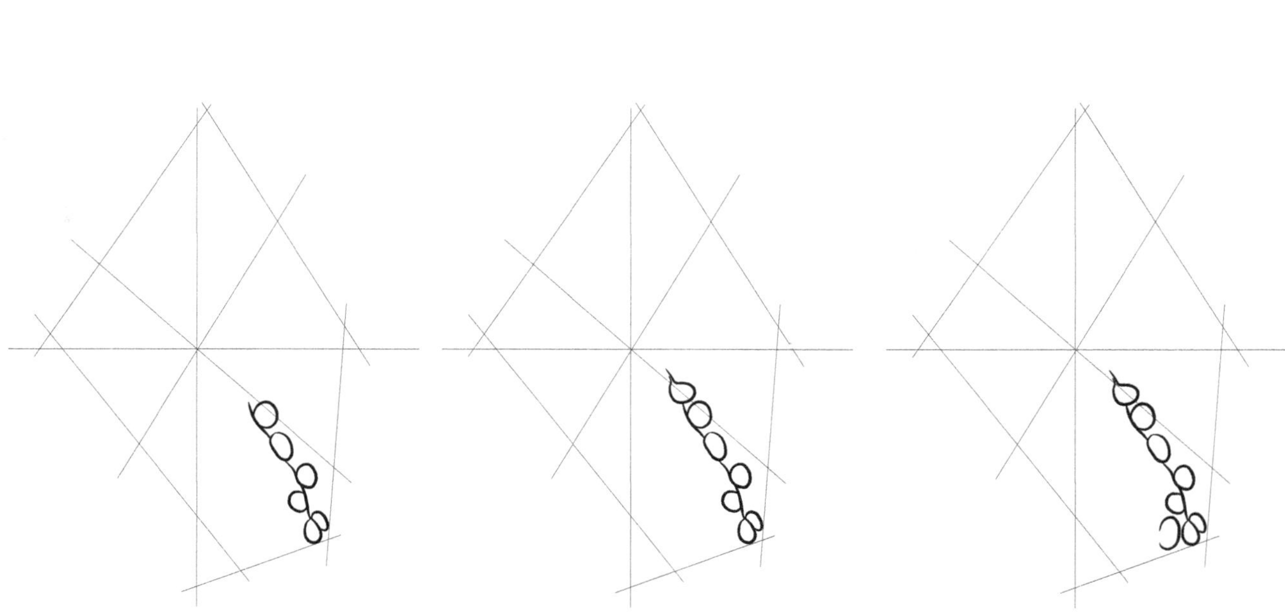

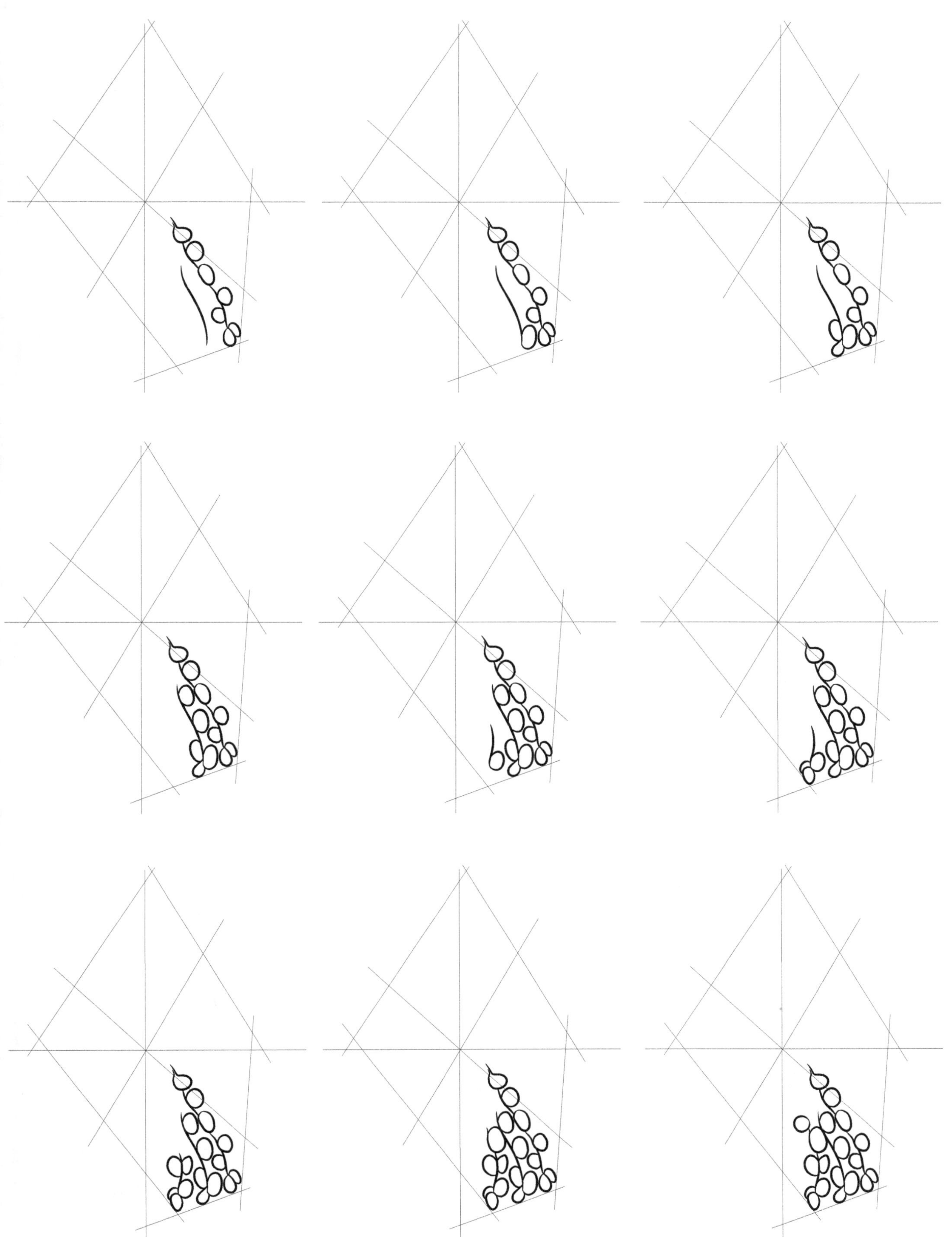

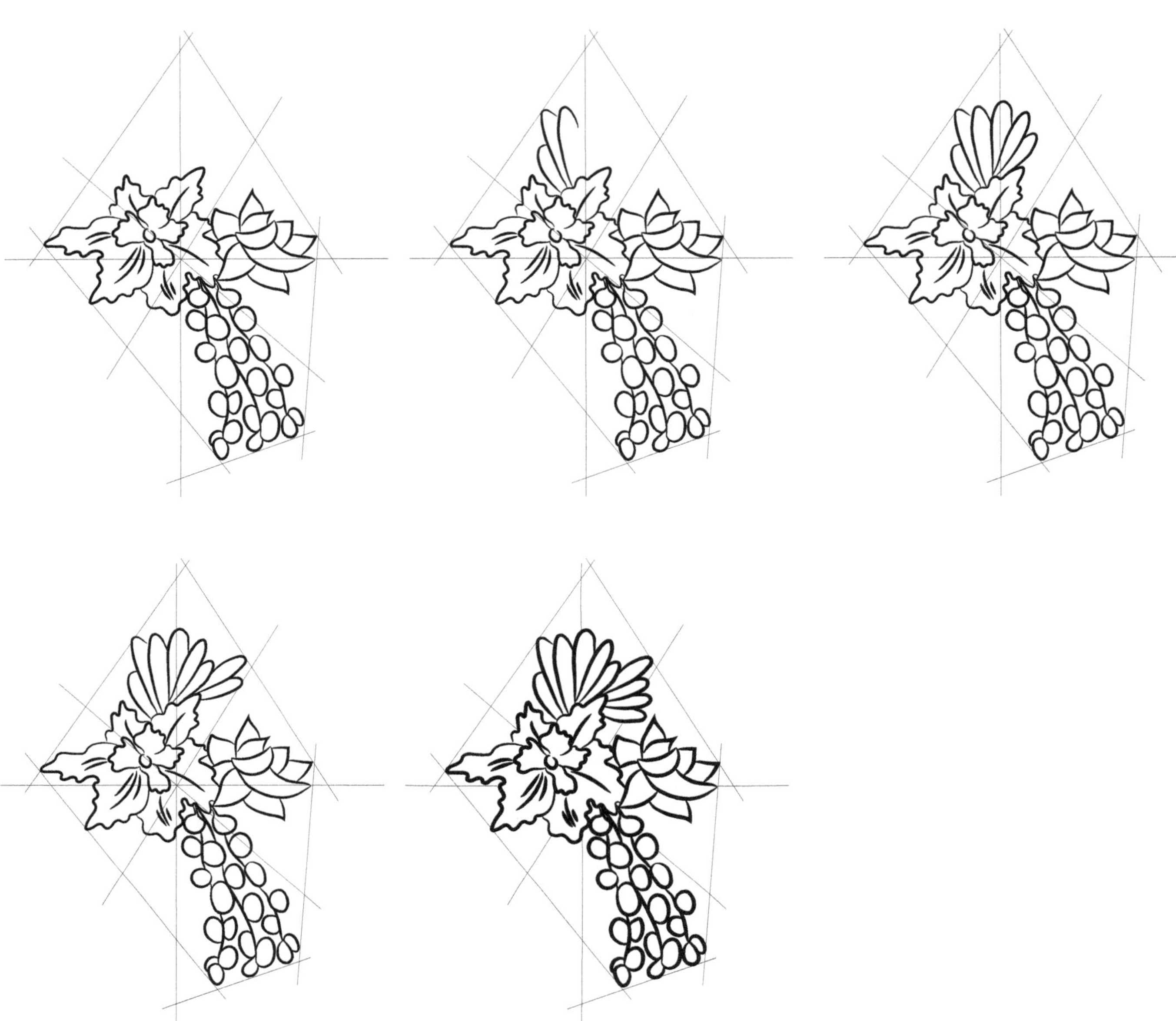

You can download blank grids to practice with in dark and light PDF formats by following the link below.

https://www.lipdf.com/product/grids/

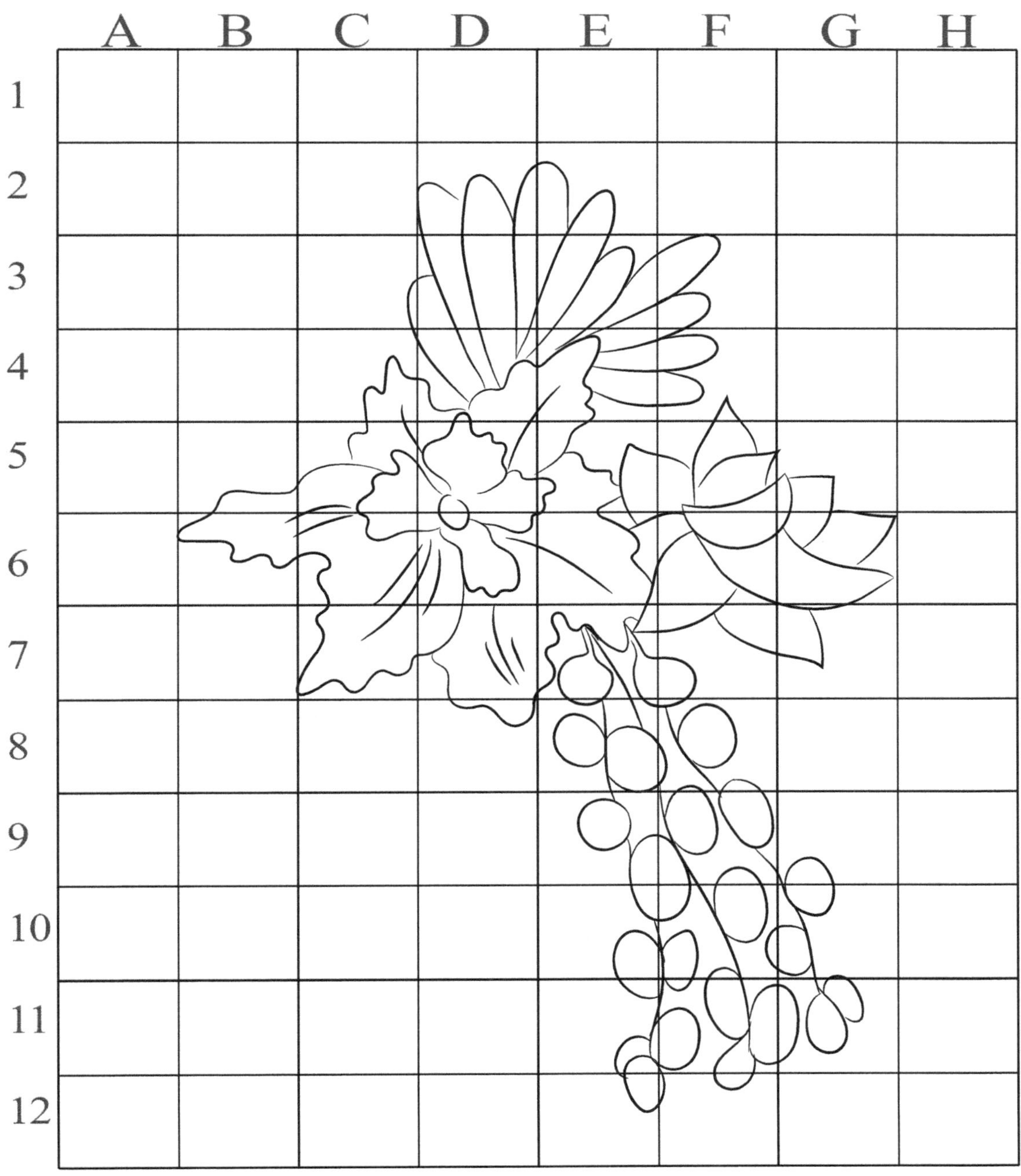

CPSIA information can be obtained
at www.ICGtesting.com
Printed in the USA
BVHW061854280121
599006BV00023B/2958

9 781800 276413